Men-at-Arms • 516

World War II Vichy French Security Troops

Stephen Cullen • Illustrated by Mark Stacey

Series editor Martin Windrow

Osprey Publishing
c/o Bloomsbury Publishing Plc
PO Box 883, Oxford, OX1 9PL, UK
Or:
c/o Bloomsbury Publishing Inc
1385 Broadway, 5th Floor, New York, NY 10018, USA
E-mail: info@ospreypublishing.com

www.ospreypublishing.com

OSPREY is a trademark of Osprey Publishing Ltd, a division of Bloomsbury
Publishing Plc.

First published in Great Britain in 2018

A CIP catalogue record for this book is available from the British Library

ISBN: PB: 9781472827753
ePub: 9781472827746
ePDF: 9781472827739
XML: 9781472827722

18 19 20 21 22   10 9 8 7 6 5 4 3 2 1

Editor: Martin Windrow
Index by Mark Swift
Typeset in Helvetica Neue and ITC New Baskerville
Originated by PDQ Digital Media Solutions, Bungay, UK
Printed in China through World Print Ltd

Osprey Publishing supports the Woodland Trust, the UK's leading woodland
conservation charity. Between 2014 and 2018 our donations are being spent on
their Centenary Woods project in the UK.

To find out more about our authors and books, visit **www.ospreypublishing.com**.
Here you will find extracts, author interviews, details of forthcoming events, and
the option to sign up for our newsletter.

ARTIST'S NOTE

Readers may care to note that the original paintings from which the colour
plates in this book were prepared are available for private sale. All reproduction
copyright whatsoever is retained by the Publisher. All enquiries should be
addressed to:

Mark Stacey, Penpont, Lanteglos-by-Fowey, Cornwall PL23 1NQ, UK

The Publishers regret that they can enter into no correspondence upon
this matter.

	Abbreviations of organizations mentioned in the text:
CSR	*Comité Secret d'action Révolutionnaire*, a.k.a. '*la Cagoule*': fascist terror group active 1935–37.
GMR	*Groupes Mobiles de Réserve*: public-order and security force founded July 1941 within *Police Nationale*, and independent from April 1943.
GP	*Groupes de Protection*: armed groups active in second half of 1940 under Vichy Ministry of War.
LF	*Ligue Française*: fascist movement founded 1940 by Pierre Constantini.
LFC	*Légion Francaise des Combattants*: ex-soldiers' organization founded 1940 by Vichy government.
LNP	*Légion Nationale Populaire*: para-military element of RNP (q.v.); became –
LSR	*Légion Sociale Révolutionnaire* within MRF/2 (q.v.).
LVF	*Légion des Volontaires Français*: volunteer military regiment that served with German Army on Eastern Front 1941–43; later absorbed into Waffen-SS.
MNP	*Milices Nationales Populaires*: short-lived para-military element of RNP (q.v. – not to be confused with *Milice Française*).
MRF/1	*Milice Révolutionnaire Français*: para-military element of LF (q.v.), founded July 1943 (not to be confused with *Milice Française*).
MRF/2	*Mouvement Révolutionnaire Française*: title adopted by relaunched MSR (q.v.) in September 1943.
MSR	*Mouvement Social Révolutionnaire*: fascist movement founded September 1940 by Eugène Deloncle, with many former members of CSR (q.v.); amalgamated with RNP (q.v.) early 1941; relaunched October 1941; renamed MRF/2 (q.v.) September 1943.
PPF	*Parti Populaire Français*: fascist movement founded June 1936 by ex-Communist Jacques Doriot.
RNP	*Rassemblement National Populaire*: fascist movement founded January 1941 by Marcel Déat.
SO	*Service d'Ordre*: para-military element of PPF (q.v.).
SOL	*Service d'Ordre Légionnaire*: para-military element of LFC (q.v.), founded January 1942 by Joseph Darnand; became *Milice Française*, January 1943.

WORLD WAR II VICHY FRENCH SECURITY TROOPS

INTRODUCTION

The Fall of France and the creation of the Vichy regime

On 10 May 1940 the German armed forces opened their assault on Western Europe. Within days the Netherlands and Belgium had capitulated, and by 4 June the British Expeditionary Force (BEF) had been bundled out of France. With the removal of the BEF from their right flank, the Germans began the second stage of their attacks on the French Army, which still had some 60 divisions in the field. On 14 June the Germans entered Paris, and two days later the French Premier, Paul Reynaud, handed power to a group led by the chief-of-staff Gen Maxime Weygand and including the long-retired 84-year-old Marshal Philippe Pétain, a heroic figure of the Great War. The next day, 17 June, Pétain broadcast to the French people that he had agreed to lead a new government, and that he intended to ask Germany for an armistice. The Armistice was signed on 22 June, and the greater part of France was formally under German occupation three days later.

The Occupied Zone covered the north and much of the centre of the country, and the whole Atlantic seaboard. In the east, Alsace and Lorraine were incorporated into the German Reich, while parts of northern France were governed from German-occupied Belgium. In addition, Italy (which had opportunistically declared war on France on 10 June) would later occupy areas on the Franco-Italian border. The remainder of metropolitan France was under the control of the new Vichy government, and was known as the 'Free' or Unoccupied Zone. In addition, most of France's overseas colonies declared for Vichy.

The events of June 1940 saw not only the division of metropolitan France, but also the creation of a new system of government. Marshal Pétain's position as the unchallenged head of a new 'French State', ruled by an authoritarian regime based in the town of Vichy, was given legitimacy by the deputies and senators of the former Third Republic. On 10 July 1940 the French people's elected representatives voted overwhelmingly to give full powers to Pétain.

Bugler of the Milice training school in the Rue d'Auteuil, Paris XVI, in March 1944. On the shoulder strap of his police-blue M1941 uniform his rank of *chef de dizaine* (squad leader) is indicated by a single white chevron. The bugle banner is embroidered with 'FRANC-GARDE PERMANENTE', a regional heraldic badge, and a unit number, '3'. (Roger-Viollet/Topfoto)

'Le Maréchal' believed that he had a paternal mission to restore the vitality and morality of France and its people, and he initiated a programme for 'National Renovation' which came to be more commonly known as the 'National Revolution'. Its watchwords were '*Travail, Famille, Patrie*' – 'Work, Family, Homeland' – and to this end the Vichy government set out to strengthen what it saw as the values of 'eternal France'. These were embodied by the Catholic church, the peasant family, and the bonds between the land and its people. Those who opposed this vision of France were, in the Vichy government's eyes, Communists, atheists, Freemasons, and the Jewish community. The domestic policy of Vichy was matched by its external policy, which – particularly in the hands of Pétain's *de facto* head of government, Pierre Laval – involved increasing collaboration with Nazi Germany, in addition to maintaining the French Empire for Vichy.

In keeping with the anti-democratic model adopted by Pétain, political parties were banned in the Unoccupied Zone. Instead, Vichy attempted to integrate all political activity under one Pétainist movement. Given Pétain's reputation as a saviour of France in World War I, the obvious base for the new movement was seen to be ex-servicemen. The resulting organization, the *Légion Française des Combattants* (LFC), incorporated veterans of the Great War, then men who had fought in the 1940 campaign, and, finally, younger men aligned with Vichy. The LFC existed in the Unoccupied Zone of France and throughout the Empire, and within a few months of its foundation in August 1940 it had a membership of 1.2 million. This mass organization was tasked with being 'the eyes and ears' of Pétain, and its main political role was to rally support for his new regime. The French Legion of Combatants also undertook extensive welfare work for the families of the 1.5 million French prisoners of war held by Germany, for old people, and for the poor in general. Initially there was widespread support for Pétain, and huge crowds attended his rallies during tours of the Unoccupied Zone. The Marshal was seen as a benevolent father-figure who had the experience and the capability to enable France to weather the storm. The Vichy regime's first year proved to be a honeymoon period, which enabled it to introduce the reforms, and repressions, that it saw as necessary for its National Revolution.

Despite the unity of purpose proclaimed by Pétain, France was in fact riven by divisions that would, over the next four years, transform it into a country at war with itself. Divisions in French society prior to the war already ran very deep. Many

A poster for the Légion Française des Combattants (LFC), intended to be the political footsoldiers of the Pétainist 'National Revolution'. Two variants of the LFC's flag are shown, both with the movement's central shield, helmet and sword device: between two conventional *tricolores* is that based on the older monarchist flag with a white cross on a field quartered in blue and red – see Plate A1. (Alamy)

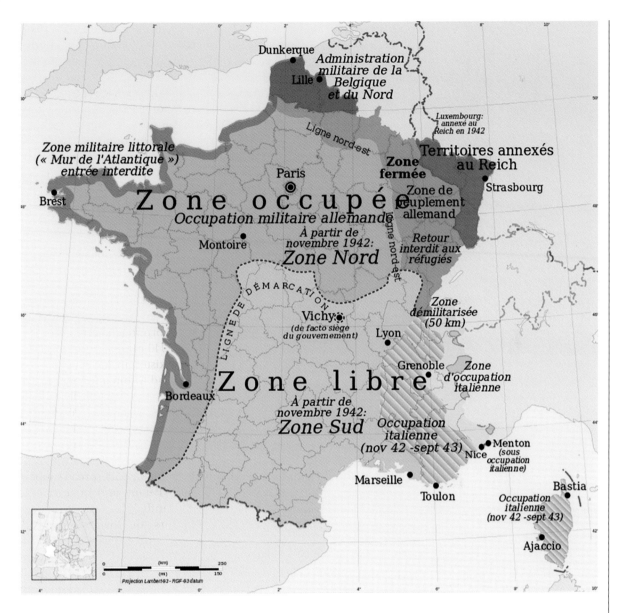

The map shows the following labels:

Dunkerque

Administration militaire de la Belgique et du Nord

Lille

Ligne nord-est

Luxembourg: annexé au Reich en 1942

Zone militaire littorale («Mur de l'Atlantique») entrée interdite

Zone fermée

Territoires annexés au Reich

Paris

Brest

Z o n e   o c c u p é e
Occupation militaire allemande

Zone de peuplement allemand

Strasbourg

À partir de novembre 1942:
Zone Nord

Montoire

Retour interdit aux réfugiés

Ligne nord-est

DÉMARCATION

LIGNE DE

Zone démilitarisée (50 km)

Vichy
(de facto siège du gouvernement)

Lyon

Grenoble

Zone d'occupation italienne

Z o n e   l i b r e

Bordeaux

À partir de novembre 1942:
Zone Sud

Occupation italienne (nov 42 -sept 43)

Nice

Menton *(sous occupation italienne)*

Marseille

Toulon

Bastia

Occupation italienne (nov 42 -sept 43)

Ajaccio

(km) 250 / (ms) 150 / Projection Lambert-93 - RGF-93 datum

saw the Left–Right struggles of the 1930s, and (in Vichy) particularly the left-wing Popular Front period of 1936–38, as the source of the defeat in 1940. Deeper still ran divisions between the secular, Republican element in the population and the Catholic, monarchist tradition. It was these divisions that Vichy sought to reconcile or eradicate, and a major part in that effort would be played by a reformed police force.

Policing and security

The Vichy government inherited a number of different police and security organizations, but also created new forces of its own. An internal Vichy assessment of the total numbers of security and police personnel available to it across the whole of metropolitan France on 10 June 1944 showed that the regime had 122,617 personnel under its control. This number was drawn from nine separate police and security forces, and included those in what had been both the Occupied and Unoccupied

The armistices signed by France in June 1940 saw the country divided between German occupation in the north and west, and Vichy's unoccupied 'Free Zone' in the centre and south. German and Italian occupation was extended over the 'Free Zone' following the Allied landings in French North Africa in November 1942, and German occupation over the former Italian zone after the fall of Mussolini and Italy's capitulation to the Allies in September 1943. (Wikipedia, France map Lambert-93 with regions and departments-blank.svg)

A member of the Gendarmerie photographed in 1943–44, after this militarized police force had been taken over by the Vichy Ministry of the Interior. As a branch of the Army it had fielded combat units in 1940, and thereafter its numbers had been strictly limited by the German occupiers; following the Allied landings in 1944 many gendarmes fought with the Free French. This M1943 uniform features a *képi* and an open-collar *vareuse* tunic in dark police-blue, and M1941 *culottes* in lighter mid-blue with a broad police-blue sidestripe. Just visible above the cuffs are his silver double chevrons of rank, and his kite-shaped collar patches bear the Gendarmerie's silver 'flaming shell' badge below upper edge-piping. The leather gaiters and belt are black.

Zones (the latter having been occupied in its turn in November 1942, following the French Army's failure to mount sustained resistance to the Allied Operation 'Torch' in French North Africa). Of that total, 54,528 personnel were mustered in four main police and security forces that had been created by Vichy. These were the *Police Nationale*, with 29,183 personnel; the *Groupes Mobiles de Réserve*, with 11,617; the *Gardes des Communications*, with 7,033; and the *Francs-gardes de la Milice Française*, with 6,695 (soon to be boosted by 8,000 more mobilized *Miliciens*).

The remaining personnel were part of police and military security forces that predated Vichy, and thus were seen by the Vichy government as less reliable. The largest of these pre-Vichy forces was the *Gendarmerie Départementale*, a nationwide organization which mustered 36,606 men on 10 June 1944. However, although it was nominally answerable to the Vichy Ministry of the Interior, the Gendarmerie still regarded itself as being part of the French Army which had been disbanded by the Germans in November 1942, and it was regarded by the regime with (justifiable) mistrust.

The focus of this book is on the Vichy-created security and police forces that were seen to be instruments of the National Revolution, and that were tasked with opposing the Resistance, defending the infrastructure of Vichy, and implementing the regime's policies in metropolitan France.

POLICE NATIONALE

The Vichy government carried out reforms of policing that were designed to increase central control, modernize organization, ensure loyalty, and strengthen and defend the regime. In addition, the reforms aimed to enhance the status and prestige of the police, making the new, updated service a model of Vichy's National Revolution. Reforms focused not just on the uniformed police, but also created a series of secret police units tasked with hounding Jews, Communists, Freemasons, and other supposedly subversive elements of the population. These organizations are outside the scope of this book, however; the focus here is on the uniformed police and security organizations created by the Vichy state, as well as non-state movements which also fought against the Resistance.

Under the Third Republic policing had largely been under the control of local government in the regional *départements*. Under Law No. 1803 of 21 April 1941 a new national force was created, the *Police Nationale*. The new force's remit covered both the Unoccupied and Occupied Zones, although not all of its elements were to be found in the Occupied Zone. The Police Nationale was organized hierarchically at county, district and regional levels, with the regional Prefects answerable directly to the Ministry of the Interior. As initially established, the Police Nationale was composed of three arms. The first of these was represented by the officers and men of the uniformed police. Known as *gardiens de la paix*, these were the everyday face of the Vichy state, present in all towns and cities throughout France. The second element were the *Police de Sûreté*, responsible for investigation, surveillance, intelligence, and combating political crimes against Vichy. Finally, under decrees passed on 23 April and 7 July 1941, a new mobile reserve was created. This was the *Groupes Mobiles de Réserve* (GMR), an integral part of the Police Nationale until

April 1943, when it gained independent status (see below). The GMR would prove to be the most effective anti-Resistance force at Vichy's disposal, and, until the regime's final days, was among the most loyal of its security organizations.

Police roles

The Police Nationale represented a sustained attempt by the Vichy state to create a police force that was loyal to the new regime. All members of the Police Nationale, whether their police careers predated the new service or whether they were newly recruited, took an oath of allegiance to Pétain as the head of state: 'I swear loyalty to the person of the head of state, and promise to obey him in whatever he commands, for the good of the service and the success of France.' Officers unwilling to take the oath were dismissed, as were those who were Jewish or Freemasons. As the war progressed, and particularly in 1944, the oath proved, for many policemen, to be a powerful brake on their abandoning Vichy and switching allegiance to the Free French.

Recruiting poster for Vichy's new 'elite' Police Nationale, created by a law of 21 April 1941. The image is that of a *commandant de 2e classe* of the Gardiens de la Paix – compare the black uniform with silver and police-blue distinctions with that illustrated as Plate C1.

The Police Nationale carried out all the usual tasks of a civic police force, but, under Vichy, enforcing a range of repressive laws became an increasingly important aspect of its role. The police were heavily involved in implementing Vichy's anti-Jewish legislation, and took part in mass arrests of Jews in both the Occupied and Unoccupied Zones for deportation to Nazi concentration and death camps. The most infamous of these police operations took place in Paris on 16–17 July 1942, when over 13,000 Jews were arrested, including some 4,000 children. They were held at the Vélodrome d'Hiver stadium in Paris in harsh conditions, as well as in the camps run by the police at Drancy, Pithiviers and Beaune-la-Rolande, and were subsequently loaded onto trains to Auschwitz. Vichy French anti-Jewish legislation and activity preceded any Nazi demands for the arrest, deportation and murder of Jews.

The Police Nationale also saw its surveillance and intelligence role expanded as the Resistance gradually became more significant. Pierre Laval, on his return to the Vichy government in April 1942 (due to German pressure), enhanced central control over the police. He appointed René Bousquet to the post of General Secretary of the Police, with powers to issue orders on behalf of Pétain. The Police Nationale also had their remit extended in the Unoccupied Zone to developing an intelligence database focused on all categories of the Resistance, foreigners and Jews.

In addition to its police and security functions, the Police Nationale had an important propaganda role for the Vichy state. The force was presented as being dynamic, modern and representing the best of French youth. Organized sport played a key part in the National Revolution's attempts to revitalize France, and the police, like the French Armistice Army, had sport integrated into their training and service. Propaganda posters, newsreels and radio broadcasts all pushed the modern, youthful, dynamic image of the Police Nationale. Recruiting posters for the force bore slogans such as '*Jeune. Moderne. Sportive*' ('Young. Modern. Sporty').

Interestingly, French women first served in the police under Vichy. From the beginning of 1944 women were recruited as uniformed 'female

GMR men pose with their transport; note the lion's-head symbol painted on the door of the lorry, and worn as a metal badge on his left upper sleeve by the right-hand policeman. All wear nine-button M1936 uniform in police-blue with a closed fall collar. Three display a unit badge, one on his right pocket and the other two in the correct position above the pocket.

agents', women *gardiennes*, or auxiliaries. They wore dark blue tunics, knee-length skirts and berets, displaying Police Nationale badges.

Police uniforms and insignia

As a standard-bearer of the new France, the new national police service was given new uniforms and insignia. These uniforms differed for officers and enlisted men.

Officers (equivalent to Army commissioned ranks) were issued with an all-black uniform with an open, notched collar exposing a light blue shirt and black necktie. All insignia reflected the installation of the new 'French State' (*l'État Français*) in place of the former Third Republic. Officers wore a peaked (visored) *casquette* cap displaying the Police Nationale badge and other silver trim, with a black band for commissioner and inspector ranks and a contrasting police-blue band for *commandants* and *officiers de paix*. Commissioners, inspectors, commandants and *officiers de paix* wore a single-breasted M1936 police tunic, and straight-legged trousers or M1936 *culottes* (semi-breeches), in black wool cloth of a good quality, with twin stripes in police-blue on the outside leg – the '*bandes de commandement*'. The tunic had shoulder straps, two pleated patch breast pockets with scalloped, buttoned flaps, and two patch skirt pockets with straight buttoned flaps. Rank badges were worn on the cuffs, horizontally for senior ranks in the form of a police-blue *barrette* featuring silver representations of acanthus leaves or flowers. The four most senior ranks – three classes of principal commissioner, and that of divisional commissioner – featured combinations of stars and sprays of acanthus (see insignia chart on page 45). Junior officers, of the ranks of *officiers de paix* and *commandants* (of which there were six and three classes respectively), displayed their rank on vertically placed cuff *barrettes*, and/ or on a *barrette* above the right breast pocket. Rank was also indicated by details of the cap's silver false chin straps.

In May 1944 rank badges were modified and simplified, with the junior officer and commandant

A Groupe Mobile de Réserve motorcycle-combination team, posing with one of the 5,000 Indian Model 340 'Chief' bikes supplied to France early in 1940 by that American manufacturer. The GMR lion's-head is displayed on the sidecar, and note that its rider is armed with a captured British Sten sub-machine gun, dating the photo to 1943 at the earliest.

The majority of the GMR men grouped around their officer in this posed photograph wear Army M1941 khaki uniforms; the white gloves and gauntlets suggest that the occasion was a parade. Second left, the inverted double chevron with blue in-fill just visible above the gauntlet marks the rank of *gardien de la paix* (compare with Plate D2). The officer (centre) seems to have the horizontal rank bars of the May 1944 regulations above his cuffs, while the *brigadiers* on the right wear M1936 police-blue uniforms with gold cuff stripes.

ranks being displayed as bars above the tunic cuffs. For example, what had been three different combinations of acanthus leaves and stars for the three classes of commandant became three short horizontal bars. For a while during May–June 1944 some officers wore a combination of rank bars and acanthus leaves as an intermediate stage between old and new rank badges. How widely the 1944 pattern rank badges were actually worn by the Vichy police is unclear, but from pictorial evidence it seems that relatively few officers adopted them.

The service badges of the Police Nationale combined stylized branches of acanthus leaves with the ubiquitous symbol of the État Français, the *francisque*. This combined the *fasces* symbol of ancient Rome and Italy's Fascist Party – the bound bundle of rods – with a double-bladed axe to symbolize the fighting spirit of ancient Gaul. The *francisque* symbol, flanked by two acanthus branches (the spiky leaves symbolizing sin and punishment), featured on the Police Nationale cap badge, collar patches and tunic buttons. The collar badges were worked in bullion thread or white on black or police-blue fields. In addition, all ranks wore an octagonal metal pin-back badge (60mm deep) on the right breast pocket, featuring the *francisque*, acanthus branches, and the legend 'POLICE NATIONALE'. Policemen were also issued with the M1926 version of the Adrian helmet, painted black or police-blue, with the crest of the helmet sometimes coloured silver. The helmet badge in painted metal featured a *francisque* on a *tricolore* shield of blue, white and red.

The rank and file were issued with uniforms of dark police-blue wool. Their single-breasted M1936 Police tunic had a closed fall collar, shoulder straps, two chest pockets each with a single-button flap, and two ' slash' skirt pockets with plain slanting flaps. The tunic had nine buttons in bright aluminium finish, featuring the *francisque* and acanthus branches. The tunic could be worn with straight-legged police-blue trousers, or M1936 *culottes* with black gaiters. Like their officers, the enlisted men displayed the Police Nationale badge on the right chest pocket, and (embroidered in white) on collar patches. In addition to the basic rank of *gardien de la paix* (equivalent to a British police constable), there were four non-commissioned ranks: *brigadiers*

Although this photo of GMR policemen is of poor quality, it is interesting for the variety of weapons carried. Apart from rifles or carbines, several have Sten guns; two in the centre carry rare examples of the Thompson M1928 SMG; and at front left and right are 8mm M1914 Hotchkiss machine guns on tripod mounts. All these men wear Adrian helmets with the Police badge, and apart from one (second row, third from right) with a brown leather *blouson*, they all wear M1941 Army khaki uniforms with GMR insignia. Three in the centre show the single rank bar of probationary *gardiens de la paix stagiaires* under the May 1944 regulations, while the rest display the former double and single chevrons of *gardiens* and *gardiens stagiaires* respectively. Compare with Plates C3 and D2.

1st and 2nd class, and *brigadiers-chef* 1st and 2nd class. Rank was displayed above the tunic cuffs, and on the issue képi. *Gardiens* wore plain police-blue képis, and plain tunic cuffs. *Brigadiers* 2nd class had a single line of gold piping around the top of the képi, and a single stripe of gold braid around the tunic cuffs. *Brigadiers* 1st class displayed an additional 6cm-long stripe of gold braid on the cuffs. *Brigadier-chefs* 2nd class wore the single braids on the képi and cuff in silver, and *brigadiers-chefs* 1st class wore two silver braids in both positions.

GROUPES MOBILES DE RÉSERVE

The need for a reserve to support the French police in maintaining public order dated back to the 19th century. That role had initially been fulfilled by the Army's Gendarmerie, in particular by its *Garde Républicaine Mobile*, which was founded in 1921 and was some 21,000 strong in 1940. However, about 5,000 gendarmes operating in military roles were taken prisoner by the Germans during the May–June campaign, and, like other French PoWs, these were only released very slowly. Further, the Gendarmerie, as part of the Army, were limited by the Armistice to only six regiments in metropolitan France, amounting to some 6,000 men. The Mobile Republican Guard was disbanded in November 1940, part of its personnel being transferred to the Departmental Gendarmerie, and about 6,000 being used to form in the Unoccupied Zone a new force, *la Garde*; this also had six 'legions', later renamed regiments.

The Garde's status changed following the German occupation of the remainder of the country in November 1942, when Vichy brought the Gendamerie under the control of the Ministry of the Interior. As already remarked, the former Army status of the Gendarmerie led to its being regarded with some distrust, and as the security situation deteriorated in early 1944 the Gendarmerie, and particularly the Garde, suffered from many desertions to the Resistance. From the beginning, instead of relying on the Gendarmerie, Vichy had taken the opportunity, with the creation of its new Police Nationale, to build upon a pre-existing model of a well-equipped, well-trained mobile police force to support the civil power. This model was the *Réserve Mobile* – six units of a small force created in 1937 for the Seine-et-Oise region.

Using this forerunner as a pilot scheme, the *Groupes Mobiles de Réserve* (GMR) was created as an element within the new Police Nationale by a decree of 7 July 1941. The GMR would prove to be Vichy's most effective, best-equipped and most loyal security force for most of the existence of the État Français. (After the fall of Vichy the Liberation government transformed the GMR, by the addition of Free French personnel, into the famous *Compagnies Républicaines de Sécurité* (CRS), which still today carry out the same public order and mobile reserve functions for the French police.)

Organization and establishment

The initial plan was to establish 180 GMR groups across metropolitan France; however, only 87 operational groups plus a number of training schools were established by the summer of 1944 (see table overleaf). Of those, 64 groups were based in the Unoccupied Zone, since the Germans initially forbade the deployment of the GMR in the Occupied Zone. However, following unrest in the Occupied Zone in the summer of 1942 the German authorities agreed that the GMR could be deployed there, albeit equipped only with sidearms, and eventually 23 groups were located in the North. Of the total of 87 groups, only 70 were fully operational by the summer of 1944.

Each standard GMR group was of company strength, led by a *commandant*, with four *officiers de paix*, four *brigadiers-chefs*, 17 *brigadiers*, 21 *sous-brigadiers* and 170 *gardiens*, plus an attached medical officer and administrative personnel. In addition, eight GMR groups in the Unoccupied Zone were mounted or mixed horse-and-motorcycle units (Groups 48, 49, 60, 61, 70, 71, 80 and 81). These groups had reduced establishments of a *commandant*, four *officiers de paix*, four *brigadiers-chefs*, 12 *brigadiers*, 16 *sous-brigadiers* and 113 *gardiens*.

The GMR organization was quickly established in the Unoccupied Zone, and within a few months of its creation it mustered nearly 7,000 men. This total consisted of 32 *commandants*, 126 *officiers de paix*, 126 *brigadiers-chefs*, 504 *brigadiers*, 6,048 *gardiens*, plus 32 supernumerary *brigadiers* and 63 administrative *gardiens*. As the numbers of groups grew so the force became more effective, achieving wider geographic coverage. By June 1944 the GMR mustered over 11,600 men in the 64 groups based in what had been the Unoccupied Zone and the 23 groups in the former Occupied Zone. Nevertheless, this fell short of an authorized establishment of 15,822 of all ranks.

GMR uniforms and insignia

As an integral part of the Police Nationale until April 1943, when it became an independent force, the GMR shared the same basic uniform. GMR commissioned officers wore the all-black uniform with a white shirt and black necktie, and straight-leg trousers or *culottes* with two sidestripes in police-blue. The enlisted ranks' uniform was the M1936 Police pattern in police-blue, with a light blue shirt and black tie. All ranks could wear the police képi, but in practice most GMR officers wore the soft-top peaked cap while enlisted ranks more usually wore a large ' Alpine'-style beret in police-blue.

These black or dark blue uniforms were not particularly well suited to the field operations in which the GMR increasingly became involved, and in 1943 the first adaptation to GMR uniform appeared. This was the introduction of a 'windcheater'-type *blouson* jacket in brown leather to replace the tunic, this typically being worn with the *culottes* in police-blue and long black leather gaiters. The leather jacket was similar in cut to that issued, particularly in mountainous areas, to units of the Vichy youth organization, the *Chantiers de la Jeunesse*, and may, in fact, have been the same garment. The issue of the leather *blouson* was an intermediate step in the development of a practical field uniform, and in the spring of 1944 one began to be issued in khaki wool cloth. This was the Army's M1941 uniform, but worn with the police-blue beret or the M1926 helmet. With this field uniform both officers and enlisted ranks could wear a khaki shirt and necktie. The National Police's *francisque*-and-acanthus collar patches were added to the tunic.

Rank insignia worn by the GMR prior to May 1944 were much the same as for the National Police, with some specific differences, but from that month a second-pattern rank system took the form of gold bars (*barrettes*) above the tunic cuffs: for example, one for an *officier de paix*, two for an *officier de paix principal*, three for a *commandant*. Non-commissioned second-pattern ranks were displayed as inverted yellow chevrons above the cuff: for example, one chevron for a probationary *gardien stagiaire*, and two for a *gardien*. The new rank insignia were most frequently worn on the khaki M1941 field uniform issued from 1944.

In addition to rank insignia and the Police Nationale's collar and breast badges, members of the GMR also displayed their own famous lion's-head insignia on the upper left sleeve of the tunic. This was a circular badge in white (or for enlisted ranks, sometimes bronze) metal featuring the head of a roaring lion in left profile; the badge was also painted on the trucks and equipment of the GMR. (The details of the badge resembled that of the German anti-Communist Freikorps von Epp of 1919, and there was a widespread belief that this German Freikorps unit badge was the inspiration for the GMR insignia.)

The second GMR-specific badge worn by its members was a unit identifier, worn centred above the right breast pocket of the tunic. These were shield-shaped pin-on badges in painted or enamelled metal, displaying heraldic designs linked to each unit's area of operations. For example, that of GMR No. 13 'Île de France' featured three gold *fleur-des-lys* on a blue field, while the shield of GMR No. 5 'Bretagne' featured Brittany's famous black-on-white heraldic ermine motif.

GMR weapons and equipment

The GMR was equipped to carry out the mobile support role, with trucks, cars and motorcycles to ensure mobility. This gave the force a high degree of flexibility, and, compared with other security units (and the French Resistance) it provided an important 'force multiplier' element for the GMR. In addition, there were the seven mounted GMR units, as well as a mixed mounted and motorcycle unit based at Vichy itself as the Groupe Mixte Ministériel, with specific protection duties in the capital of the French State.

The GMR were issued with a range of French arms and, unlike the *Milice* (see below) did not have to resort to using weapons from a variety of sources. Among the types of handgun issued were the ubiquitous old 8mm M1892 revolver, the 7.65mm Ruby semi-automatic (copied very widely since 1914 from the Browning M1903), and the 7.65mm M1935 and M1935S service semi-automatics. Issued rifles included the old 8mm Lebel M1886/93 and Berthier *mousqueton* M1892/1916, along with the standard French Army 7.5mm MAS36. The GMR had some .45in Thompson sub-machine guns, and – courtesy of captured Royal Air Force drops to the Resistance – very many more 9mm Sten guns. The Army's standard 7.5mm FM 24/29 light machine gun was issued, and heavier support was provided by the 8mm Hotchkiss M1914 machine gun and the 60mm Brandt M1935 mortar.

GMR operations

The GMR was a barracked force, in the tradition of other similar organizations such as the Spanish Guardia Civil or the Royal Irish Constabulary. Its training was focused on maintaining public order and carrying out military action against armed groups, in both urban and rural

These two GMR motorcyclists wear black M1933 crash helmets with the National Police badge, and apparently brown leather M1935 mechanized troops' three-quarter length coats over police-blue uniforms; they carry slung MAS36 rifles. They are checking the papers of a civilian lucky enough to own a 1934 front-wheel-drive Citroen 'Traction-Avant', the car of choice for both police and gangsters.

environments. Its most important role was in the 'anti-terrorist' struggle against the Resistance, which saw it carrying out a wide range of activities. Its core tasks were disrupting Resistance cells by military action and arrests; intelligence-gathering; the suppression of Resistance publications; the interception of air-drops of arms and equipment by the RAF, and the capture of Allied airmen and agents; and the arrest of Jews, and of workers attempting to avoid the compulsory labour draft to Germany.

As the war progressed and armed resistance grew, so the GMR's functions expanded. From August 1943, GMR officers sat on special courts before which captured Resistants were brought for trial and sentencing. When the Armistice Army was disbanded after the German invasion of the former Unoccupied Zone in November 1942, the GMR were given the new task of providing firing squads for Resistants who had been condemned to death. As the fighting between Vichy and its opponents reached a peak in the summer of 1944, so GMR firing squads found themselves executing compatriots who had been condemned by 'kangaroo' courts conducted by the ultra-collaborationist Milice.

The GMR took part in some major military operations against the Resistance, sometimes in conjunction with the Milice and German forces. One of the most notable of these was the 'Battle of Glières', 31 January–26 March 1944. The success of the GMR and German security units in intercepting RAF arms drops was compounded in the aftermath of the disbandment of the Armistice Army by the speed with which the GMR secured Army arms depots. British Special Operations Executive (SOE) agents were sent to identify and establish secure areas where the Resistance could receive weapons and equipment, and one of these was the Glières plateau in the mountainous Haute-Savoie region of south-east France bordering both Switzerland and Italy. The commanding officer of the local *Maquis* ('the scrub' or 'bush' – the popular nickname for the Resistance) was Théodose 'Tom' Morel, a former French Army lieutenant who had been decorated for bravery in the 1940 campaign. His initial orders were to collect parachute drops from the RAF on the plateau, but local attacks by the Germans led to the decision to establish a permanent stronghold at Glières. The Vichy authorities responded by declaring a 'state of siege' in Haute-Savoie, which meant that anyone found carrying weapons or assisting the Maquis in any way was liable to immediate court-martial and execution.

The GMR, supported by 800 *Miliciens* and some gendarmes of La Garde, began offensive operations, and the *maquisards* retreated onto the plateau itself. Eventually Morel had some 450 maquisards at Glières, where the RAF dropped 30 supply containers of arms and munitions. The newly supplied Maquis now faced about 2,000 GMR and Milice, and clashes soon intensified in difficult mountainous terrain in bad winter weather. Eventually a GMR officer agreed to a temporary truce and discussion of a prisoner exchange. The Maquis accused the GMR of having broken the terms agreed, and responded on the night of 9/10 March with an attack by more than 100 men on buildings occupied by GMR No. 28 'Aquitaine' in the village of Entremont at the foot of the plateau. The party led by Morel captured GMR officers in the Hôtel de France, but Cdt Lefebvre hotly refused an offer of negotiation with 'bandits' and, pulling a concealed pistol, he shot Morel dead (and was himself immediately shot). The fighting resumed, and became more savage when the bodies of captured and executed GMR men were found. The RAF were able to make more air-drops during March, but then the Germans intervened; air attacks were followed, on 26 March, by an advance by some 4,000 men including three battalions from 157. Reserve Infanterie-Division and two German Polizei battalions, supported by artillery and armoured cars. The Maquis were forced to retreat, suffering many casualties killed outright or captured, to be interrogated under torture before execution or deportation to concentration camps.

The inability of Vichy security forces to suppress the Glières Maquis without major German support illustrated their limitations by early 1944, but set-piece confrontations such as that at Glières, and at Vercors in June–July 1944, were the exception. Typically the GMR and other Vichy units faced traditional hit-and-run guerrilla tactics, along with targeted assassinations. The GMR was much more effective in countering this type of opposition, at least before the Allied landings in Normandy in June 1944 and in Provence in August led to the final collapse of the Vichy state.

OTHER VICHY ORGANIZATIONS:

Groupes de Protection

The Vichy government attempted to convey an impression that all of France was united behind Pétain and the National Revolution. However, not only was the regime faced, from the outset, with hostility from fascist and ultra-collaborationist groups based in Paris, but there were also divisions within Vichy's own ranks. Not least of these was the personal animosity between Pétain himself and the long-time 'independent socialist' Pierre Laval. In addition, many of the key players in Vichy, while officially Pétainist, had strong political affiliations stemming from the inter-war period, and there was much in-fighting between different factions each attempting to impose their version of the National Revolution. Early in the French State's existence a group of officers linked to the Vichy Minister of War, Gen Huntziger, established the first political security unit at Vichy itself, the *Groupes de Protection*.

The Protection Groups first appeared in public in Lyon in October 1940, parading at an anti-Freemasonry exhibition in the city. This unit had been formed weeks earlier under the command of Col Georges Groussard, who answered to Gen Huntziger and the Vichy Interior Minister, Marcel Peyrouton. Groussard would later, in the summer of 1941, travel to London to attempt to persuade the British government to reach an agreement with Vichy; he was arrested on his return, subsequently joining the Resistance as an intelligence agent. Groussard's wartime career is an illustration of how figures who were initially supporters of Vichy moved towards resistance, as the Vichy regime moved towards closer collaboration with Germany.

Men of Marshal Pétain's personal Guard on parade in Vichy, June 1944. Apart from their navy-blue *culottes*, they wear the same uniform and equipment as illustrated in Plate D3. (Roger-Viollet/TopFoto)

The Groupes de Protection was a security force tasked with suppressing opposition to the Vichy government – whether from those outside the regime, or those within it who were suspected of being less than wholly supportive of Pétain. The force was a cross between a 'commando' and a secret police, not unlike the character of the early German SS within the mass SA movement. The basic unit was the *groupe* of 12 men plus an officer, with three *groupes* forming a *section*, and four *sections* forming a *compagnie*, with a combined roll of 160 plus a company headquarters. Groups were established across the towns and cities of the Unoccupied Zone, with concentrations in Lyon, Marseille, Nîmes, Toulon and Nice, and were fully equipped with cars, motorcycles and motorcycle combinations. Each *groupe* of 13 men was armed with handguns, sub-machine guns, grenades and an FM1924/29 light machine gun. The Groupes de Protection mainly operated in plain clothes, but some also received uniforms. The issue headgear was the M1935 pattern motorized troops' helmet, with a flat leather frontal pad and a wide leather face-piece incorporating the chin strap; it was finished in khaki, but bore no arm-of-service badge. Both officers and enlisted ranks wore the three-quarter length M1935 armoured troops' leather coat in brown leather, and 1922/41 pattern mounted *culottes* in khaki wool, worn with high gaiters. The only insignia displayed was a white brassard worn on the left arm, featuring a black disc with the letters 'GP' embroidered in mixed gold and red thread (see Plate A2).

The members of the Groupes de Protection were recruited from among former and serving military personnel, and also from the ranks of a pre-war fascist terror group, the *Comité Secret d'action Révolutionnaire* (CSR), more commonly known as *la Cagoule*, which had been founded by Eugène Deloncle. Former members of the CSR would provide leadership and militants not only for Vichy, but also for separate fascist groups in occupied Paris, and even for the Free French. Their prior experience of underground activity and terrorism, combined with their military training, made the Groupes particularly effective: for example, in the weeks before Pétain visited Marseille in November 1940 the GP effectively destroyed the French Communist Party (PCF) in that city, 'neutralizing' some 8,000 members and suspects.

The Germans were uneasy about the Groupes de Protection, fearing (correctly) that many members of this secretive armed organization were as strongly anti-German as they were anti-Communist. On 13 December 1940 the Groupes de Protection took part in raids in Vichy itself, during which Pierre Laval was removed from office and arrested in the course of an internal power-struggle in the Vichy government. The Germans, who regarded Laval as their most useful ally in external collaboration between France and Germany, protested; Laval was released, eventually returning to his post as premier in April 1942. The Laval crisis gave the Germans the excuse they needed to demand the disbandment of the Groupes de Protection, which was announced on 22 December 1940.

La Garde du Maréchal

Pétain's personal Marshal's Guard was formed in August 1942, and was operational by that October. It had both protection and ceremonial duties, and consisted of 559 officers and enlisted ranks drawn from ex-members of the former Republican Guard and Mobile Guards. The Garde du Maréchal was commanded by Col Barre, and was answerable to the Gendarmerie; as such it was a military police formation, despite being a creation of the Vichy government. Its personnel were most commonly seen on guard duty outside government buildings in Vichy, including the Hôtel du Parc where Pétain had his private residence, and they also accompanied him at public events. They were a visible expression of the Vichy state, so their standard of turn-out and drill was high. In addition, the Garde du Maréchal was complemented by a ceremonial military band, the *Musique de la Garde Personnelle du Chef de l'État*, consisting of 109 musicians under a *chef de musique*. This was present at all official Vichy state events, and performed frequently for Vichy radio broadcasts.

The Marshal's Guard was issued with four uniforms: two for parade duty, and one each for guard and everyday duty. Ceremonial uniform included bicorne hats displaying a cockade and ribbon in French colours. More usually, officers and men wore Gendarmerie uniforms. When on sentry, escort and protection duties personnel wore a version of Army motorized troops' uniform. Headgear was the M1933 motorcyclists' helmet, painted gloss black and displaying a special enamelled metal badge (see commentary to Plate D3). A black version of the M1935

Gardes des Communications posing for a group snapshot on a railway platform, wearing a variety of uniform and non-uniform clothing; compare with Plate D1. (Left) a non-standard uniform, apparently in khaki. (Second & third from left) regulation navy-blue *surveillance* tunics, one with beret, *culottes* and gaiters, the other with *casquette*, visible green collar and cuff insignia, and straight trousers. (Centre) officer with non-regulation open-collar tunic, showing cuff tab of a *sous-chef* or *chef de secteur*. (Third from right, & far right) civilian shirts, jackets and ties. (Second from right) as second from left. All seem to wear the GdC badge on tunics and/or headgear.

17

leather motorcyclists' coat, single-breasted and with a closed *demi-saxe* fall collar, was worn over the police tunic, with black leather *culottes*, long gaiters and boots, and a belt with a special white-metal buckle. On sentry duty the Gardes du Maréchal were normally armed with a revolver and the Berthier M1892/1916 carbine.

Gardes des Communications

The protection of key transport links became increasingly important as the war progressed and the Resistance grew more active. The first priority was to ensure the security of the rail network, and in January 1941 the first *Gardes des Communications* were appointed, answerable to the Secretary of State for Communications in Vichy. At first the Communications Guards operated only in the Unoccupied Zone, but the need to protect the railways against sabotage increased, and in October 1941 their operations were extended to include parts of the Occupied Zone. By March 1942 the force was operating in the Paris region, and in May control of the Gardes des Communications passed to the Vichy Secretary General of Police, bringing the force more clearly into the security and policing apparatus. In some areas the Gardes des Communications were supported, from April 1943, by a part-time militia recruited from men aged 18–50, who had a night-watchman role. The Communications Guards were responsible for the protection of bridges, tunnels, stations, marshalling yards and the points at rail intersections, in addition to general surveillance and policing tasks. In June 1944 the force had 3,706 personnel operational in what had been the Occupied Zone, along with 3,327 in the former Unoccupied Zone; these numbers were rather fewer than the authorized establishment of 8,490 officers and men.

The Gardes des Communications were issued a uniform in navy-blue wool; this consisted of a five-button, single-breasted, closed-collar tunic known as a *surveillance*, worn with matching *culottes* or straight-legged trousers. Senior ranks wore peaked *casquettes* and junior ranks berets. The force's distinctive colour was mid-green, displayed as plain shoulder straps and trouser seam piping. Special rank insignia were displayed on collar patches and as tabs on the cuffs (see chart, page 45). On a green backing, these bore respectively the service's 'GC' monogram in red, and a sequence of rank 'stars' in red, white and yellow, the rank classes also being differentiated with red, white and yellow edge-piping. Much of the clothing was of economy materials and cut, with even the issue greatcoat (*capote*) being single-breasted. In shirtsleeve order a white cloth brassard was worn on the left upper arm, featuring the Gardes des Communications' insignia of a white vertical dagger superimposed on a white gearwheel on a black shield topped with a tricolour bar. This badge was also worn on headgear, including the M1926 helmet issued for patrolling, which was painted midnight blue or black.

The Gardes des Communications were armed with sidearms and rifles, but their effectiveness was variable; though they had an important role, they were essentially a passive area-security force. As armed resistance grew in the build-up to the Allied landings the GdC became less reliable and effective. The rail system was heavily targeted by the Allied air forces as well as by the saboteurs of the energized Resistance, and, especially after the Normandy landings, individual members of the force deserted to join the Free French.

THE PARIS 'ULTRAS'

Political factions and their militias

The Franco-German Armistice left Paris inside the Occupied Zone. During the collapse the French government had relocated first to Bordeaux, and then, following the transfer of power to Pétain, to Vichy. The Vichy regime had no room for political parties, equating them with the fractures and divisions that Vichy argued had led to the débâcle of May–June 1940. As already mentioned, Vichy promoted its Légion Française des Combattants (LFC) as a pseudo-political movement that was loyal to Pétain and was intended to mobilize support for the National Revolution. Paris, by contrast, saw the growth of political parties of the ultra-right, some of them pre-dating the war, others emerging under the Occupation. These parties and their militias were banned from organizing in the Unoccupied Zone, although various 'cultural associations' were formed there which had links to the Parisian groups. Paris thus became the centre of collaborationist political parties which, to one degree or another, acted as rivals to the Vichy regime. Their ideological antagonisms were of a bewildering variety, but any account of anti-Resistance groups active under the Occupation must include a basic listing. (A mass of acronyms is sadly unavoidable – readers may find it helpful to cross-check with the glossary on page 2.)

The rivalries between the Paris ultra-collaborationists and the Vichy government did not, however, entirely preclude co-operation between the two, since there were personal and political ties between Paris-based collaborators and those in Vichy. For example, the prominent Paris-based leader Marcel Déat, who had been a socialist member of the inter-war French parliament, had a number of contacts with Vichy officials who had sat with him in the National Assembly. Déat's wartime movement, the *Rassemblement National Populaire* (RNP), had an active para-military organization, the *Légion Nationale Populaire* (LNP), which was built around supporters of the Cagoule pre-war terrorist group (see above). The key Vichy supporter and founder of the Milice, Joseph Darnand, had

A rally of the Parti Populaire Français at the Vélodrome d'Hiver stadium in Paris, August 1943. This occasion symbolizes the para-militarization of collaborationist politics; the militiaman in the foreground wears a dark blue uniform with the PPF brassard. Under magnification it is possible to make out among the men in the crowd, mostly wearing the party's blue shirt, some individuals in German Army uniform with the armshield of the Légion des Volontaires Français. The 'Vél d'Hiv' was the scene of many such rallies, but was also used to assemble Jewish detainees before they were transported to Nazi concentration camps. (Roger-Viollet/TopFoto)

Members of a fascist party and of the Milice stand by a cordon of the Police Nationale. The young militant giving the fascist salute wears the blue shirt and red necktie of the Rassemblement National Populaire (RNP), with black trousers cut in the popular 'ski' pattern – compare with Plate B1. Over his tunic the policeman with the baton wears the little-worn cape thrown back over his shoulders; note that the police helmets have silver crests. (Bundesarchiv, Bild 101I-719-0236-17/photo: Wörner)

belonged to the Cagoule, along with other Vichy activists including members of the Groupes de Protection. These connections became even more significant after the Germans occupied the whole country in November 1942. Vichy security operations were then further extended into the North, and the ultra-collaborationists in Vichy and Paris worked together in the armed struggle against the Resistance. The focus here is on those movements based in Paris which had active para-military organizations, whose members increasingly bore arms as the war progressed.

Parti Populaire Français

The Parti Populaire Français (PPF) was founded in June 1936 by the former Communist Party luminary Jacques Doriot. Known as 'le Grand Jacques' because of his height and manner, Doriot was once described by Grigory Zinoviev, the head of the Communist International, as a model Bolshevik. Doriot made the working-class area of Saint-Denis in Paris into a Communist stronghold, and even after his expulsion from the French Communist Party (PCF), and the creation of his fascist PPF, Saint-Denis continued to provide him with a strong base of support. (Readers puzzled by this apparent contradiction may reflect that both Communists and Fascists shared a similar critique of capitalism and parliamentary politics, and also a belief in totalitarian solutions to society's problems.) A veteran of the Great War, Doriot also fought in the 1940 campaign, winning a second Croix de Guerre. Later he would serve alongside the Wehrmacht on the Eastern Front with the *Légion des Volontaires Français* (LVF) – which was, in part, his brainchild. The PPF aimed to become the premier collaborationist movement, and harboured dreams of forming a potential government in place of the Vichy regime, but Doriot's absence from France during three tours on the Eastern Front did little to further its ambitions.

The PPF was one of the largest pre-war fascist parties in France, with 137,000 members in 1937, around a third of whom had followed Doriot from the Communist Party. The PPF was composed of numerous sections, including uniformed para-militaries who, under the German Occupation, extended their pre-war struggle with opponents. PPF militants infiltrated Resistance groups; identified and denounced Jews, Freemasons and Communists; and carried on a low-level campaign of political violence. As the war developed and the Resistance grew stronger, so the PPF was increasingly targeted for assassinations; in six weeks during June and July 1944 there were some 7,000 armed attacks on collaborationists, including many PPF members.

The PPF's main uniformed para-military groups were the *Service d'Ordre*, the *Gardes Françaises* and the *Groupes d'Action*. The Service d'Ordre was the PPF's basic para-military organization. Consisting of an active element and a reserve, it was organized as two separate groups in the Occupied and the Unoccupied Zones; in the latter it was a tolerated but unofficial group. Normally, the militants of the Service d'Ordre were not uniformed, but at all PPF events such as rallies and parades they wore a dark blue uniform consisting of a sidecap, a double-breasted *blouson* jacket over a pale blue shirt, and straight-legged or ski-type trousers. In addition, they were identified by a special brassard. The standard PPF brassard featured an octagonal badge in red with the initials 'PPF' in white, on a red, blue and white field, the white being a narrow saltire. The Service d'Ordre brassard also featured the letters 'S' and 'O' on either side of the central PPF octagon. In the Occupied Zone the German authorities were unwilling to allow para-military groups to be armed, but as the Resistance grew, and particularly following the German occupation of the remainder of France, it became clear that fascist party militants needed to be armed for self protection. Even as early as September 1942 the Service d'Ordre headquarters in Paris was damaged in a grenade attack which killed and injured a number of militants. At first they were limited to small-calibre handguns, though by 1944 this had been relaxed.

The *Gardes Françaises* were formed by the PPF in November 1942. Growing ever closer to the Nazi political model, Doriot intended that the French Guards should be a sort of French Allgemeine-SS, while the PPF's Service d'Ordre would mirror the Nazi Sturmabteilung (SA). The Gardes Françaises were composed of young men and women from within the party, chosen as an elite and supposedly able to prove pure French ancestry. They were nominally organized in combat sections, companies, battalions and divisions. A combat 'section' was made up of 12 men; three sections made a 'company'; four companies formed a 'battalion', and ten battalions formed a 'division' of nearly 1,500 Gardes. Women were organized in separate sections, as were youngsters.

The first commander of the Gardes Françaises was a retired Army officer, LtCol Paul-Marie Gamory-Dubordeau. A veteran of the French Foreign Legion, and a long-time member of the PPF, Gamory-Dubordeau went on to be the first commanding officer of the Französische SS-Freiwilligen Sturmbrigade. This embryonic Waffen-SS unit started recruiting in the spring of 1943, in parallel with the German Army's LVF regiment; by 30 September over 1,500 Frenchmen had volunteered, though only around one-third of these were accepted. Interestingly, a survey of recruits carried out in December 1943 showed that 20 per cent were from the PPF, and it is likely that most of those came from the Gardes Françaises. (The various fascist parties based in Paris, particularly the PPF, provided a stream of recruits to various German military and auxiliary formations.) The Gardes Françaises wore the PPF's blue shirt, but with a dark blue brassard, edged red, bearing the PPF's unique Celtic-cross-cum-*francisque* symbol on a white octagonal field edged red.

The *Groupes d'Action* were formed in 1943 specifically to protect and support PPF members, their families, and those of Frenchmen serving on the Eastern Front, from attacks by the Resistance. The first Action Groups were formed in the Unoccupied Zone, then extended to the North; eventually nine Groupes d'Action were formed, in Blois, Cannes, Clermont-Ferrand, Épinal, Grenoble, Lyon, Nantes, Nice and Toulouse. Members wore a blue uniform, and were armed with sidearms and sub-machine guns.

Mouvement Social Révolutionnaire/ Mouvement Révolutionnaire Français

The Mouvement Social Révolutionnaire (MSR) was the creation of Eugène Deloncle, the pre-war leader of the fascist terror group, the *Comité Secret*

Young militants of various fascist parties in Paris taking part in a recruiting drive for the volunteer Workers' Committee for Immediate Assistance, part of the movement's air-raid support efforts. (There was a real need for this: Allied bombing of France would eventually kill some 60,000 civilians). The two youngsters at left wear the red brassard of the **Légion Nationale Populaire (LNP)**, bearing a black stylized *gamma* like a reversed *Odalrune* on a white diamond (see Plate B1). The youth in the middle wears two brassards; the upper one is that of the combined Jeunesse Populaire Française movement (see Plate B2).

d'action Révolutionnaire (CSR – 'la Cagoule'). Founded in 1935, that group's aim was to destabilize the French political system and to combat Communism. Organized on military lines, it undertook sabotage and assassinations, and smuggled tons of weapons into France. The Cagoule was dealt a major blow in 1937, when much of its underground organization was rolled up by the police.

During the war, veterans of the Cagoule allied themselves with all sides in the conflict – with Vichy, the Paris-based 'ultras', and even the Gaullists. Deloncle relaunched his movement as the MSR in September 1940, and many of his old comrades rallied to him. However, in January 1941 Marcel Déat formed a new movement, the *Rassemblement National Populaire* (RNP – see below). Recognizing that Déat was much more of a politician than he was, Deloncle threw his lot in with the RNP. Following the German invasion of the Soviet Union in June 1941 the Paris-based parties created the Legion of French Volunteers (LVF) to fight alongside the Germans, and during the first months of recruiting the largest number of politically committed volunteers came from the ranks of the former MSR. This was an indicator of how action-focused the para-military MSR supporters were; it was former MSR militants who, with the acquiescence of some elements in the German occupying forces, burnt down seven Parisian synagogues during the night of 3/4 October 1941. The relations between Déat and Deloncle were already strained, and these actions led to a final rift.

Deloncle re-founded the MSR, taking many of his old supporters with him, but his enthusiasm for collaboration was waning, and he began to make contacts with Gaullists. This led to a Gestapo raid in November 1943, when Deloncle and his son were killed in a shoot-out. However, despite the gradual withdrawal of Deloncle from his movement, the MSR itself continued under a seven-strong leadership committee, who changed the movement's title to *Mouvement Révolutionnaire Français* (MRF) in September 1943.

In both guises, the movement ran a number of para-military uniformed sections which were active against Resistance enemies and fascist rivals. The MSR had around 8,000 members in Paris and the same number in other areas of the Occupied Zone. The movement's militia was called the *Légion Nationale Populaire* (LNP) while it was part of the RNP in 1941. The LNP lost many of its most active members to the LVF and the Eastern Front, but it was still an active anti-Resistance militia. It was organized in so-called squads, sections, battalions, groups and brigades, with some 162 sections in six brigades in Paris.

After the break with the RNP, the LNP changed its title to the *Légion Sociale Révolutionnaire* (LSR). The LNP/LSR operated a number of sub-sections, two of which – the *Sections d'Intervention Différée* (SID), and the *Section Spéciale* (SS) – were particularly active against the Resistance. In addition, Deloncle had a bodyguard composed of White Russians and other non-French anti-Communists. The basic uniform of the MSR was a dark blue shirt, black trousers, beret and necktie. Officers wore open-necked tunics in dark blue, with *culottes*, boots and 'Sam Browne' belt. The movement only adopted a party badge after the split with the RNP. The first pattern MSR badge, worn on the tunic or shirt pocket, featured a hand clutching an upright sword in white on a blue and red field, with the letters 'MSR', and on the sword's crossguard the motto 'Aime & Sers' ('Love & Serve'). The second-pattern badge featured a bronze sword bearing that motto, or 'MSR', superimposed on two concentric circles in red.

Rassemblement National Populaire

The *Rassemblement National Populaire* (RNP – 'National Popular Rally') was, as already mentioned, the wartime creation of Marcel Déat, a long-time socialist deputy (member of parliament) and a veteran of the Great War. Formed in February 1941, the RNP grew to around 300,000 members by the summer of that year. This rapid growth, and the political leadership of Déat, made the movement the main rival to Doriot's PPF. The RNP quickly established its own militia, the *Milices Nationales Populaires* (MNP), for propaganda and security purposes; but with the RNP's absorption of the MSR that party's existing militia, the LNP, became its main fighting force. By the summer of 1941 the RNP claimed that it had six brigades of LNP in Paris, with a total of 10,000 LNP militants throughout France. This was undoubtedly an exaggerated figure; however, at the combined fascist parties' rally held at the Vélodrome d'Hiver in Paris on 18 July 1941 to create the LVF for service in Russia, the RNP's LNP fielded 2,042 uniformed militants compared with just 101 provided by the PPF. Subsequently the RNP, like the other fascist parties, lost many of its most active men to the meatgrinder of the Eastern Front, thereby weakening the movement in France.

The LNP was the spearhead of the movement, and under its leader, the heavily decorated veteran Paul Montagnon, it sought to 'serve and carry out the orders of the Chief [Déat], for the glory of the Party, for France, and for European socialism'. LNP officers wore a dark blue uniform of open-necked tunic, shirt, necktie, *culottes*, boots and beret. Enlisted ranks wore a work shirt in mid-blue with a red tie. The LNP brassard worn on the left arm was red, with a printed white diamond showing an angular black *gamma* fashioned to resemble a partial swastika (actually, it was an upside-down *Odalrune*). On the left breast pocket of tunics and shirts the 'horseshoe and flames' metal badge of the RNP was worn. As with the other militias, the LNP became increasingly involved in clashes with the Resistance, and began to carry small-calibre sidearms.

Recruiting office for the LVF in Charenton, May 1944; although the title is unchanged here, by this date the survivors of the Army formation were being absorbed into the Waffen-SS. Such obvious targets for the Resistance now had to be protected, and the bureau is guarded by uniformed militiamen (probably from the PPF) armed with captured Sten guns.

Ligue Française

Among the other movements and groups based in Paris, the *Ligue Française* (LF – 'French League') operated a uniformed militia whose origins lay in armed service with German military and auxiliary units. The League was founded by a famous French airman, Pierre Constantini, who served in both world wars. Anti-Communist and anti-British, Constantini adopted a strongly collaborationist policy. In July 1943 the LF announced that it was forming a new militia to combat the Resistance and protect the movement; this was named the *Milice Révolutionnaire Française* (MRF – not to be confused with the *Mouvement Révolutionnaire Français*, described above). Members of this 'second' MRF were drawn from former French military personnel and, importantly, from Frenchmen who had already served on the Eastern Front with the LVF, the NSKK Nazi transport corps, or the Organisation Todt labour and construction organization. The MRF wore an all-black uniform including tunic, trousers, shirt and necktie, with a French *tricolore* arm shield embroidered with 'MRF' on the upper left sleeve. Shoulder straps were piped white, and some personnel sported death's-head badges. Closely associated with the Sicherheitsdienst (SD) in Paris, the MRF were armed from the outset, and in some areas personnel came under direct SD control in their war with the Resistance. This was the case in Dijon in February 1944, when the local MRF was reinforced from Paris, and the enlarged unit was subsequently issued with SD uniform by the Germans.

MILICE FRANÇAISE

The Pétainist Légion Française des Combattants (LFC) was never the dynamic movement that the Vichy government hoped it would be when it was created in August 1940. Although it quickly enrolled very large numbers of ex-servicemen sworn to defend the new *État Français*, most of these men lacked much commitment to the principles of the National Revolution. However, one ex-soldier who did possess a militant belief in that cause was Joseph Darnand. A hero of both world wars, he had provided one of France's few good-news stories during the 'Phoney War' of 1939/40. Darnand's aggressive patrolling during that winter had made him a national hero, and he appeared on the cover of the famous magazine *Paris Match* in March 1940, photographed after receiving another gallantry medal to add to those he had received in World War I.

(continued on page 33)

THE VICHY 'NATIONAL REVOLUTION'
1: *Légion Française des Combattants*, 1942
2: *Groupes de Protection*, 1941
3: *Chef de dizaine, Service d'Ordre Légionnaire*, 1942

A

THE PARIS 'ULTRAS'
1: *Légion Nationale Populaire*, 1942
2: *Jeunesse Populaire Française*, 1943
3: *Milice Révolutionnaire Française*, 1943

B

GROUPES MOBILES DE RÉSERVE
1: *Officier subalterne*, 1942
2: Motorcyclist, 1943
3: *Gardien*, 1944

POLICE & SECURITY UNITS, 1942–44

1: *Sous-brigadier, Garde des Communications*, 1942
2: *Gardien, Groupes Mobiles de Réserve*, 1944
3: Motorcyclist, *Garde du Maréchal*, 1943

D

MILICE FRANÇAISE, 1943–44
1: *Franc-garde permanente*, 1944
2: Officer candidate, Uriage, 1943
3: *Franc-garde non-permanente*, 1943

MILICE FRANÇAISE, 1943–44
1: *Franc-garde permanente*, 1943
2: *Milicienne*, 1943
3: *Franc-garde permanente*, 1943/44

F

MILICE FRANÇAISE, PARIS, JULY 1944
1: *Chef de cohorte*; Les Invalides, 1 July
2: *Chef de trentaine*; Les Invalides, 1 July
3: *Chef de dizaine*; Champs-Élysées, 2 July

MILICE FRANÇAISE, JULY 1944
1: *Franc-garde permanente, Groupe Spécial de Sécurité*
2: *Chef de dizaine, Franc-gardes permanentes*, Burgundy
3: *Franc-garde permanente*, Rennes

An image that is almost cinematic in its atmosphere of drama and threat: Darnand (centre) photographed at a meeting at the Trocadéro in Paris in July 1944. He is flanked by a leather-coated bodyguard, and a uniformed officer of the Milice displaying the *gamma* right breast badge and the numeral '1' on his double-piped collar patches. (Bundesarchiv, Bild 146-1983-077-16A/photo: Kempe)

Darnand was a long-time fascist militant, and a member of the Cagoule during the late 1930s. However, he was known to be fiercely anti-German as well as anti-Semitic and anti-Communist. Although he came to symbolize the worst aspects of French collaboration with Nazi Germany, it was not a foregone conclusion that he would become an active collaborator. Others with a similar background joined the Resistance and, particularly, followed Gen de Gaulle. In fact Darnand made at least two attempts to join the Resistance, but was rebuffed. In the end his belief that the overriding threat to France was international Communism, a belief shared by many 'ultras', led him to armed collaboration and civil conflict with his compatriots.

Darnand was appointed the Regional Chief of the LFC in the department of Alpes-Maritimes. In an initiative designed to inject some revolutionary dynamism into the movement, he formed, in January 1942, a new section of the LFC called the *Service d'Ordre Légionnaire* (SOL). The SOL opened its membership not just to ex-combatants but to all those who supported the aims of the National Revolution. Darnand saw this fully fledged fascist organization as providing an elite political force to spearhead the fight for a 'New Order' in France. Despite its being initially envisaged as a political entity, increasing Resistance in both zones of France prompted the SOL's development into an auxiliary security force for the Vichy government. Active armed Resistance began to be seen by Vichy, if not yet by the German authorities, as a serious problem. In particular, the Resistance targeted members of collaborationist groups and movements, including the SOL. As a result SOL members were issued with sidearms, and fascist party members in the Occupied Zone looked to any contacts they had with the Germans in order to acquire weapons.

Against this background, on 5 January 1943 Darnand separated the SOL out from the LFC, to create the *Milice Française*; although Laval was its nominal head, Darnand was from the outset the actual leader. He

In January 1942 Joseph Darnand created – within the very large but rather inert LFC – the Service d'Ordre Légionnaire (SOL), which he intended to be a political 'ginger group'. This SOL militant wears black civilian trousers with the black beret, khaki Army shirt with buttondown collar, and black necktie that would be adopted by the Milice Française when Darnand formed it from the SOL a year later. The shoulder patch is unidentified; the black *barrette* above the right pocket bears the three gold-yellow stars of a *chef départemental*, and he wears a regional badge on his left pocket. Note too the brassard on his left arm (see Plate A3), cut in the shape also adopted by the Milice, with narrow ends buckled together on the inside of the arm.

May 1944: *Miliciens* distributing to needy families food and drink seized from 'black market' traders. By this stage of the war the Milice were routinely armed, and the central figure has a holstered revolver at his right hip. His shirt displays the ubiquitous *gamma* badge in silver-grey on black on his right pocket, and also has non-standard shoulder straps with an added facing layer bearing a single star; this is unexplained. (Roger-Viollet/TopFoto)

still saw his new creation as being essentially a political force; it boasted women's and youth sections, and carried out propaganda and social-welfare functions, but by this date there was in fact very little prospect of its making significant political progress. In keeping with its fascist nature, however, and the context in which it was created, it also had a security function. Darnand did not intend the Milice to be a mass movement like the original LFC, but envisaged it as an elite. Within a short time the Milice would provide the Vichy government with an extra security capability against the Resistance, and a highly politicized militia with which to counterbalance the factional fascist militias based in Paris.

Milice organization

By the summer of 1943 the Milice had a total membership of 30,412. Of that number, 12,945 were enrolled as *francs-gardes*, who were the armed security element of the movement. These included both full-time *francs-gardes permanentes* and part-time *francs-gardes non-permanentes*; the latter could be mobilized for specific actions, or, as in the aftermath of the Normandy landings, as part of a general mobilization. On 10 June 1944, Vichy Interior Ministry returns show that there were 415 *francs-gardes permanentes* serving in the North, and 6,280 *francs-gardes permanentes* and *non-permanentes* serving in the South. However, within a few weeks perhaps as many as 8,000 more would be mobilized, including the 700 newly embodied part-timers who paraded in Paris on 1 and 2 July 1944.

The *francs-gardes* of the Milice had their own organizational structure. The smallest Milice unit was the *main* ('hand'), of four *francs-gardes* commanded by a *chef de main*. Two *mains* formed a *dizaine* of ten men, plus a *chef de dizaine*. Three *dizaines*, totalling 33 men, were plus a *chef de trentaine* and his adjutant; together, the 35 *Miliciens* formed a *trentaine*. Three *trentaines* and a command group, all under a *chef de centaine* and his adjutant, formed a 119-man *centaine*. Three *centaines*, with the addition of a command group, a doctor and four medics, a radio section and communications section, formed a 384-man *cohorte* under a *chef de cohorte* and his adjutant.

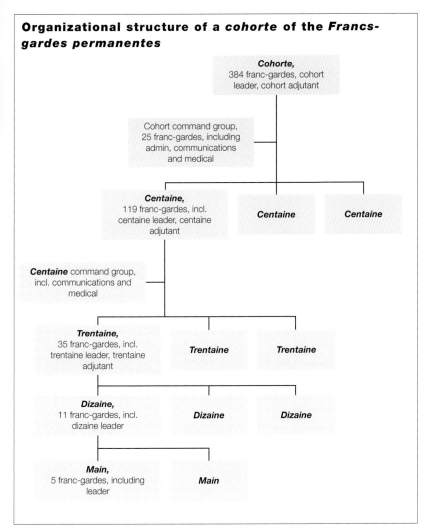

Organizational structure of a *cohorte* of the *Francs-gardes permanentes*

- **Cohorte,** 384 franc-gardes, cohort leader, cohort adjutant
- Cohort command group, 25 franc-gardes, including admin, communications and medical
- **Centaine,** 119 franc-gardes, incl. centaine leader, centaine adjutant
- **Centaine**
- **Centaine**
- **Centaine** command group, incl. communications and medical
- **Trentaine,** 35 franc-gardes, incl. trentaine leader, trentaine adjutant
- **Trentaine**
- **Trentaine**
- **Dizaine,** 11 franc-gardes, incl. dizaine leader
- **Dizaine**
- **Dizaine**
- **Main,** 5 franc-gardes, including leader
- **Main**

Milice operations

The *francs-gardes* were fully integrated into Vichy's security structure, and as Darnand became more powerful within the regime so the role of the Milice was enhanced. In October 1943 Darnand joined the SS, swearing allegiance to Hitler and being given the rank of Obersturmführer-SS (first lieutenant). In January 1944 he was appointed Secretary General for the Maintenance of Order in the Vichy government, with control of all Vichy security forces. Finally, on 24 June 1944, in the febrile, murderous atmosphere of a Resistance–Vichy civil war following the Allied landings in Normandy, Darnand was appointed Minister of the Interior.

At the operational level the *francs-gardes* typically operated alongside the GMR, or, less usually, the Garde of the Gendarmerie. For example, in 1944 the security apparatus in the Limoges region included five field units, an intelligence unit and a headquarters unit. The intelligence unit was entirely staffed by *Miliciens*, under the command of a Gendarmerie captain. The field units were mixed groups; for example, Groupement Mixte E was formed of a cohort of some 384 *franc-gardes* plus support from the GMR, while Groupement Mixte C was composed of five squadrons of the Garde, plus up to 70 *francs-gardes*. At command level,

Vichy, May 1944: Milice guard of honour at a memorial to their dead of 1943, smartly turned out in best uniforms with full insignia and decorations, black belt equipment and M1941 gaiters and boots – compare with Plate G2. (Roger-Viollet/TopFoto)

the Milice officer commanding and a colonel of the Gendarmerie operated under the political and security direction of the regional Prefect's office and the regional Director for the Maintenance of Order, who was a *Milicien* answering directly to Darnand.

The *Miliciens* were a mixture of political idealists, opportunists, adventurers and small-time criminals. They were quickly seen as being the 'ultras' of Vichy France, and were much hated and feared by the Resistance. In its operations, the Milice became known for its use of informers, torture, reprisals and extra-judicial killings. Resistance action against *Miliciens*, Vichy officials and other collaborators inevitably provoked reprisals from the Milice, often against innocent civilians. On 28 June 1944 one of the Milice's most notable members, the Vichy Secretary of State for Information, Philippe Henriot, was assassinated by members of the Maquis disguised as *Miliciens*. Henriot received a state funeral at Notre Dame Cathedral in Paris, and the Milice began a series of reprisals. These included the murder of Georges Mandel, a notable politician during the inter-war period who was a strong critic of collaboration. But the Milice also targeted others; for example, the village of Saint-Amand-Montrond suffered the arrest and deportation to concentration camps of 70 Jewish refugees. A similar example of tit-for-tat killing had occurred in the town of Voiron, near Lyon, in April 1944. The Resistance murdered the entire family of a *Milicien*, including five children, the youngest aged three months. This atrocity was naturally broadcast by Vichy for propaganda purposes, and brought new recruits for the Milice; in direct reprisal, local *francs-gardes* executed some school students whom they claimed to be involved.

The Milice was also to the fore in more purely military clashes. Its most infamous actions were the large-scale offensives against the Resistance 'stronghold' on the Glières plateau (see above), and the offensive against the Vercors Resistance in June–July 1944. But the Normandy invasion and the Allied breakouts in summer 1944 began the final act in the life of Vichy, marked by an intensification of what was essentially a civil war. Following the Allied landing in Southern France in August 1944, Vichy finally ceased to exist, with the Germans evacuating what remained of its government first to eastern France, and then to Sigmaringen in southern Germany.

Surviving *Miliciens* retreated to Sigmaringen, often in long convoys which came under repeated attack by the Resistance. Around 1,200 of those who reached Germany were later compulsorily drafted into the Waffen-SS, while Darnand and a *bataillon de marche* ended the war fighting Italian partisans around Milan. Those *Miliciens* captured in France were usually executed. Darnand was returned to France in July 1945, tried, and executed in October 1945.

Milice uniforms and insignia

As the parent organization of the Milice, the Service d'Ordre Légionnaire (SOL) provided the initial core of *Miliciens* and elements of the force's uniform. The SOL's basic dress was a khaki shirt usually of military cut, with black or dark blue trousers. Officially the trousers were supposed to have been of the 'golf' pattern in navy blue, but photographic evidence suggests that straight, full-length civilian trousers were typical. A black or dark blue beret and a black tie completed the outfit, but there was a good deal of variation. Photographs show SOL militants wearing trousers loose over ankle boots or shoes, or tucked into light-coloured socks rolled down over the top of ankle boots in hiking style. The exact shade of SOL shirts varied from a dark greenish or brownish khaki to a light sand colour. Brown leather gloves were popular, and were often worn turned

Taking a break during a training exercise at Uriage, near Grenoble in the Alps, in February 1944, these *Miliciens* have 'piled arms'. The weapons include both 7.5mm MAS36 rifles and 8mm M1892/1916 carbines, and note (centre) two 7.5mm FM1924/29 light machine guns. Pale shoulder straps identify instructors. (Roger-Viollet/ TopFoto)

February 1944: *Miliciens* presenting arms at the main entrance to the Milice leadership school at Uriage. This provided leadership candidates with both political and military instruction. (Roger-Viollet/TopFoto)

back on the cuff. The SOL brassard was worn on the left arm; it displayed a vertical sword dividing the letters 'S' and 'O' on a black shield on a white circular ground. Rank insignia took the form of a rectangular *barrette* above the right breast pocket.

With the transformation of the SOL into the Milice, and the increasing stress on the new organization's security role, its uniform reflected that development. The original plan envisaged the force being dressed in dark blue, although it has been suggested that iron-grey was also used for initial issues. Since there were never enough full uniforms to equip the whole force there were inevitably variations, most notably between the *francs-garde permanentes* and *non-permanentes* (also known as the *francs-gardes bénévoles*). Photographs show tunics with or without shoulder straps, and khaki shirts with shoulder straps but lacking breast pockets.

The initial uniform came in a winter and a summer issue. The winter version included the Army's M1941 pattern *vareuse* (tunic) but in dark police-blue. This was a four-pocket, open-collar tunic with detachable shoulder straps and two rear cuff buttons, as issued in khaki to Vichy's Armistice Army from 1941. A non-standard *blouson*-style jacket of 'mountain' type in police-blue was also issued, but was far less common than the M1941 tunic; it had an open collar and two breast pockets. The Milice inherited the SOL's khaki shirt and black necktie, along with the beret. The Milice beret was supposed to be of the large 'Alpine' or 'Fortress' pattern, pulled to the right for officers and to the left for enlisted ranks, although in practice this distinction was usually ignored. Sometimes smaller 'Breton' or civilian berets were seen, of the dimensions used by Army armoured troops.

April 1944: an armed *franc-garde permanente* escorts the funeral cortege of a (probably assassinated) militiaman in the Paris suburb of Pantin. The procession is made up of uniformed but unarmed men in shirtsleeve order, almost certainly Milice *franc-gardes non-permanentes*; several of them are clearly well past military age. (Roger-Viollet/TopFoto)

It is very hard to distinguish from photographs whether berets are in midnight blue-black or the slightly lighter police-blue, and both were almost certainly used.

The Milice's badge, worn on the beret and right breast pocket, was the Greek letter *gamma* in white metal, or machine-woven in silver-grey thread on a black disc or shield. (This character was associated with the Zodiacal Ram, a symbol of virile renewal.). The other commonly seen breast badge, often worn by Milice officers on the left pocket, was the circular *gamma*-and-sword of graduates from the Milice's military and political leadership school at Uriage. Unit collar patches were worn, by the permanent *franc-gardes* at least, bearing numerals below double-chevron piping on the short upper edges of the 'kite'-shaped patches. Some regional insignia were also seen displayed on the tunic, usually as cloth shields on the upper left sleeve. As the security situation became more critical, and especially after the full mobilization of July 1944, unit and regional insignia were frequently omitted. The rank system was represented by a sequence of chevrons and bars on the shoulder straps (see chart, page 46). The summer uniform most closely resembled that of the SOL; in addition to the dark blue trousers, khaki shirt, black tie and beret, *Miliciens* also wore a blue brassard on the left arm, bearing the *gamma* badge machine-woven on a central white disc.

The Milice were also issued with the Armistice Army's M1941 straight trousers, again in police-blue, either worn loose or tucked into the tall M1941 leather gaiters known as '*demi-houseaux*'. Typically, *Miliciens* wore a brown or blackened belt, usually the Army's M1903/14 with a double-claw frame buckle, and only a single rifle cartridge pouch, but 'Sam Browne' belts were also worn; either might support various types of holstered revolvers and semi-automatic pistols. In cold conditions *Miliciens* received the Army-cut M1941 greatcoat also in police-blue. They were often issued M1926 helmets; these were frequently but not invariably painted black or dark blue, and sported the *gamma* badge either stencilled in white paint or stamped from white metal.

Although the dark police-blue uniform was the initial issue, the most distinct version was that distributed from June 1944, particularly in the North, following the general mobilization of the non-permanent element. The Vichy authorities were able to equip only about half of the 8,000 newly mobilized men with the police-blue uniform, and instead at least half of the volunteers called up were issued Army M1941 khaki uniforms (which were already being worn by, amongst others, the GMR). For example, 700 newly sworn-in Paris region *francs-gardes* paraded down the Champs-Élysées on 2 July 1944 wearing the khaki uniform, prior to being sent on anti-Resistance operations. The khaki uniform was worn with the dark blue beret, detachable dark blue shoulder straps, and the *gamma* right pocket badge.

This photo supposedly shows the arrest of Resistance supects in the Vercors in July 1944, when some 4,000 *maquisards* attempting to hold ground in the mountains were crushed by German and renegade Russian and Ukrainian troops, plus 500 Milice *francs-gardes*. These militiamen wear light field order, with only a tent-cloth roll in addition to their belt kit. The man at far right wears the waist-length *blouson* alternative to the police-blue Milice tunic (see Plate F1), apparently with khaki trousers, and typically carries a Sten SMG. The fate of his prisoners is likely to be, at best, deportation to a German concentration camp. (Roger-Viollet/TopFoto)

Women in the *Milice*

The Milice inherited the SOL's political role, which (especially in the early days, before security duties became paramount) involved social relief work. One of the aims of the National Revolution was to support what Vichy called 'communal socialism'. The Milice made great play of distributing seized black-market goods, and operated communal kitchens. Food, clothes and furniture (often stolen from deported Jewish families) were distributed, in particular to families of French prisoners of war still held by the Germans, to those left homeless by Allied bombing, and to the families of dead *Miliciens*. Another target group were mothers of large families; motherhood was encouraged by the Vichy government, which introduced a range of family benefits.

Miliciennes bagging foodstuffs for distribution in the predominantly working-class Parisian district of Saint-Denis, 1944. Formerly a stronghold of the French Communist Party, it was, from the late 1930s, a key area for the fascist PPF led by Jacques Doriot, himself a former Communist leader. For the uniform worn by these women, see Plate F2. (Roger-Viollet/TopFoto)

The women's section of the Milice was known as *l'Avant-Garde feminine*, and *Miliciennes* played a prominent role in this 'direct social action'. Photographs show girls and women wearing a version of the Milice uniform consisting of the khaki shirt, black tie and dark blue beret, with a dark blue pleated skirt worn to just below the knee. Like men who were members of the Milice but not of the *francs-gardes*, women wore on the right shirt pocket a *gamma* badge in silver on a royal-blue disc with double red edging.

Milice weapons

The Milice used a mixture of French, Italian, British and US small arms. At first *Miliciens* only received sidearms, largely for personal protection, but as the security situation deteriorated it became clear that they would have to be properly equipped to fight a counter-insurgency campaign. In June 1943 three cohorts (1,381 men) were mobilized at Calabres, near Vichy, and therefore needed a range of personal weapons. The problem was that the Vichy government needed the permission of the German authorities to distribute weapons held in French Army stores. At first this permission was not forthcoming, as in the summer of 1943 the Germans did not believe that the Resistance posed a sufficient threat to themselves or to lines of communication to warrant additional armed units under the control of Vichy. The Milice did, however, manage to source French weapons (from where is not entirely clear) before, on 18 August 1943, the Germans agreed to the release of French small arms. These were of standard patterns – MAS36 rifles and FM1924/29 light machine guns, in addition to various revolvers and pistols. Small numbers of Erma Vollmer MPE sub-machine guns, which had been taken from Spanish Republican troops interned in Southern France at the end of the Spanish Civil War in 1939, were also issued.

The need for more weapons became urgent once the Milice began operating in what had been the Occupied Zone, and as the Resistance threat increased in anticipation of the Western Allies' landings to begin the liberation of France. From the spring of 1943 the Milice were operating throughout the whole country, and this increased tempo of operations, culminating in full mobilization of all part-time *francs-gardes* in June 1944, put an increasing strain on Milice resources. A significant contribution was made by releasing the captured arsenal of British and US weapons, ammunition and grenades from intercepted Allied air-drops (see below). Well-known

In the courtyard that is the spiritual heart of the French military, some 1,500 *Miliciens* paraded before Darnand at Les Invalides on 1 July 1944 to re-affirm their oath of service. The ceremony was also attended by SS-Gen Oberg, the Higher SS & Police Leader for France, along with senior French figures such as Fernand de Brinon, Vichy's ambassador to Germany. The colour party wear regulation M1941 uniform – see Plate G2. (Roger-Viollet/TopFoto)

Weapons used by the *Milice*

	Weapons from French military & police armouries	Allied weapons captured from Resistance air-drops
Sidearms	8mm M1892 revolver	.38in Enfield No. 2 Mk 1* revolver
	7.65mm Ruby automatic	.45cal US M1911A1 automatic (few)
	6.35mm Unique automatic	9mm Browning No. 2 Mk 1 'Hi-Power' automatic (few)
Sub-machine guns	7.65mm MAS38 (rare)	9mm Sten Mk II (most common SMG in use)
	9mm Erma Vollmer (very rare)	9mm United Defense M42 'Marlin' (very rare)
	.45cal Thompson M1928 (very rare)	
Rifles	7.5mm MAS36	.303in SMLE No. 4 Mk I & Mk I*
	8mm *mousqueton* (carbine) M1892/1916	Various Italian carbines (rare)
		.30cal US M1 carbine (rare)
Light machine guns	7.5mm FM 1924/29	.303in Bren Mk I & Mk IM (Canadian)
Machine guns	8mm Hotchkiss M1914 (rare)	

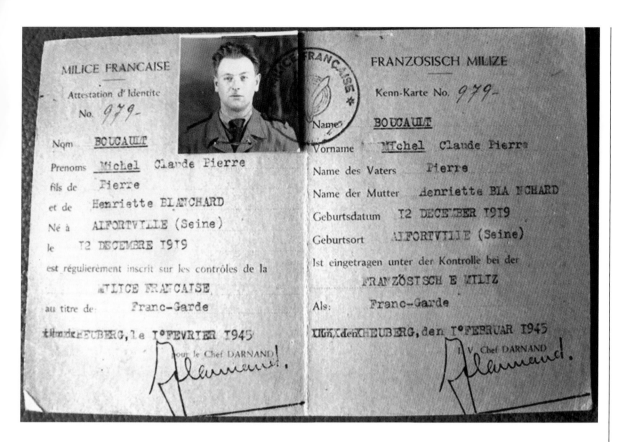

images show *Miliciens* carrying Bren light machine guns, Sten sub-machine guns and Lee-Enfield rifles, thus mirroring photographs showing members of the Resistance armed with captured German weapons. For example, sufficient Brens had been captured to allow the allocation in some Milice units of two Brens per *dizaine* (i.e. a squad of 11 men, in two five-man fire groups plus an NCO). The use of large numbers of Stens was facilitated by the wide availability of compatible 9mm ammunition.

An identity card issued to a *Milicien* in exile at Heuberg in Germany, 1 February 1945, and signed by Darnand. The holder was *Franc-Garde* Michel Boucault, 25, from Alfortville in the Seine Department; his photo shows the khaki M1941 uniform with added police-blue shoulder straps but without collar patches. Boucault may have been one of about 1,200 members of the Milice drafted into the under-strength 33. Waffen-Grenadier Division de SS 'Charlemagne', which was overwhelmed in the Pomeranian campaign of late February–March 1945.

SELECT BIBLIOGRAPHY

Abbas, Benoit, 'Les Groupes Mobiles de Réserve, 1941–1944', in *Uniformes* Nos. 286 & 287 (Paris; 2013)

Baux, Cdt Jean-Pierre, *Les Groupes Mobiles de Réserve* (privately published, Metz; 2002)

Historia Hors Série No. 40, *La Milice; la Collaboration en Uniforme* (Paris; 1975)

Historia Special No. 31, *Collaboration et collaborateurs* (Paris; September–October 1994)

Lambert, Pierre Philippe, & Le Marec, Gérard, *Organisations, Mouvements et Unités de l'État Français; Vichy 1940–1944* (Jacques Grancher, Paris; 1992)

Lambert, Pierre Philippe, & Le Marec, Gérard, *Partis et Mouvements de la Collaboration; Paris 1940–1944* (Jacques Grancher, Paris; 1993)

Lefèvre, Éric, 'Des Armes pour les Miliciens', in *Gazette des Armes* (Paris; May 1984)

Lefèvre, Éric, 'Franc-Garde de la Milice Française', in *Militaria* No. 111 (Paris; October 1994)

Lefèvre, Éric, '"À Quelques-Uns, Contre Presque Tous…"; La Milice Française de Février à Août 1943, du Malentendu à l'Impasse', in *Batailles* No. 15 (Paris; April–May 2006)

Littlejohn, David, *The Patriotic Traitors; A History of Collaboration in German Occupied Europe, 1940/1945* (Heinemann, London; 1972)

Segrétain, Franck, 'La Milice Française (1940–1945)', in *Les Dossiers de la 2e Guerre Mondiale, La France en Guerre* No. 10 (Paris; October, November & December 2007)

PLATE COMMENTARIES

A: THE VICHY 'NATIONAL REVOLUTION'

A1: *Port-étandard, Légion Française des Combattants*, August 1942

In civilian dress, this Great War veteran is identified as such by his 1914–18 Croix de Guerre with three 'mentions in despatches': two palms for citations in Army orders and one star for a citation in Corps orders. He is taking part in a second anniversary parade of the Légion Française des Combattants (LFC), and bears a 'monarchist' quartered blue and red banner with a white cross; centred on this – and on the conventional *tricolore* banners which were also used – was the LFC's badge of a romanticized 'Gallic' helmet set on a *tricolore* shield, superimposed on a broadsword **(1a)**. He also displays this as embroidered beret and metal lapel badges, and wears an LFC brassard.

A2: *Groupes de Protection*, Vichy, 1941

This member of the early Protection Groups set up by the Vichy Minister of War has received a French Army M1935 motorized troops' helmet, an M1935 armoured troops' brown leather vehicle coat, and M1922/41 mounted troops' khaki woollen *culottes* worn with knee-length gaiters over M1914 ankle boots. His organization is identified by the white brassard bearing 'GP' in mixed gold and red embroidery on a black disc. His weapon is the 7.65mm MAS38 machine pistol.

A3: *Chef de dizaine, Service d'Ordre Légionnaire*, October 1942

The Service d'Ordre Légionnaire (SOL) of the LFC set up by Joseph Darnand was composed of the more active veterans. This member wears its uniform of a small 'Basque' black beret, an M1935 French Army shirt with black necktie, and black ski-type trousers gathered at the ankle. The embroidered beret badge bears the initials 'SO' on a shield with a superimposed sword; he also wears an SOL brassard in blue, white and silver. His rank of squad leader ('chief of ten') is indicated by the single gold-yellow stripe centred on the black *barrette* above his right breast pocket. The folded-arm stance was a regulation drill position.

B: THE PARIS 'ULTRAS'

B1: *Légion Nationale Populaire*, September 1942

The Légion Nationale Populaire (LNP) was the militia of the Mouvement Social Révolutionnaire. The MSR regarded itself as a 'socialist' movement, and the uniform worn by this young militant forming part of a guard of honour reflects that. On his blue work shirt he sports a scarlet necktie; the badge of the Rassemblement Nationale Populaire political party on his left pocket; the LNP brassard in red and white, with a stylized black *gamma* symbol recalling the German *Odalrune*; and the LNP badge repeated as an enamelled tie pin. The belt and boots are blackened French Army M1903/14 and M1914 issue respectively, and the guard of honour have their black ski-type trousers gathered into short mountain gaiters of whitened canvas. At this date militiamen did not yet need to carry weapons.

B2: *Jeunes Filles Françaises* wing of *Jeunesse Populaire Française*; Paris, August 1943

The Jeunesse Populaire Française (JPF) was a fascist youth movement combining youngsters from nine different collaborationist groups, one of which was the female Jeunes Filles Françaises. This teenage girl wears a dark blue peaked (visored) cap, *blouson* jacket with domed black buttons, and unpleated skirt, with a light blue shirt and black necktie. The left sleeve badge is the white cross on a red disc of the combined JPF; the little metal badge on her left collar is that of the Union Populaire de la Jeunesse Française, the initial title of the combined movement.

B3: *Milice Révolutionnaire Française*, December 1943

The militia of the Ligue Française, the MRF recruited from French officers and from returned veterans of the Légion des Volontaires Française (LVF), the military unit that fought with the Wehrmacht on the Eastern Front from November 1941 as Reinforced Inf Regt 638. Note this ex-soldier's Croix de Guerre on the green and black LVF ribbon, the buttonhole ribbons of the German Iron Cross 2nd Class and the Russian

Studio portrait of a Police *gardien de la paix stagiaire* or probationary constable of the Groupes Mobiles de Réserve – compare with Plate D2. He wears the Army M1941 khaki uniform, with the National Police's white *francisque-and-acanthus* collar patches and the single yellow chevron of his rank, both on dark police-blue backing; note the blue 'in-fill' of the chevron. Despite his most junior rank he wears his holstered sidearm on a 'Sam Browne' belt. Note that the tunic lacks shoulder straps. The insignia on the dark blue 'Alpine' beret is unidentified, but he clearly displays a shield-shaped unit badge on his right pocket.

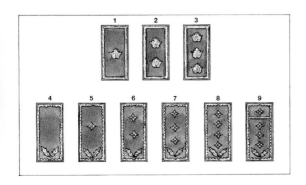

Police Nationale officers' cuff rank badges, April 1941–May 1944 – all silver on police-blue:

(1) *Officier de paix de 1ère classe*; (2) *Officier de paix hors classe*; (3) *Officier de paix principal*.

(4) *Commandant de 4e classe*; (5) *Commandant de 3e classe*; (6) *Commandant de 2e classe*; (7) *Commandant de 1ère classe*; (8) *Commandant principal de 2e classe*; (9) *Commandant principal de 1ère classe*.

(Drawings by Adam Hook)

Winter 1941/42 Medal, and the silver Wound Badge on his pocket. The tunic of his all-black uniform is a French Army M1941 *vareuse* dyed black, with added shoulder straps piped white, and the MRF sleeve patch on the left arm **(3a)**. He carries a private-purchase 6.35mm Unique pistol on his ex-French Army belt.

C: GROUPES MOBILES DE RÉSERVE
C1: *Officier subalterne*; Vichy, July 1942
This junior commissioned officer of the Vichy government's Police Nationale wears the all-black M1936 officers' uniform with a light blue shirt and black tie. His officers *casquette* cap has a silver-edged band in dark police-blue, which also appears as two 25mm-wide stripes on the side seams of his leather-reinforced riding breeches. The cap badge is the Vichy French State's emblem of a *francisque* (a double-bladed axe in a bundle of *fasces*) between stylized acanthus branches. The same motifs appear in silver bullion thread on his pentangular collar patches, and on a pierced and enamelled white-metal badge on his right breast pocket. As an officer of the GMR within the Police Nationale he displays on his left upper sleeve a white-metal badge of a lion's head in profile **(see 1a)**; the coloured enamel badge above his right breast pocket is that of his specific unit, Groupe Mobile No. 38 'Bourbonnais'. His exact rank of *officier de paix principal* is indicated by three silver stylized acanthus-leaf sprays on the silver-edged police-blue strip on each cuff.

C2: Motorcyclist; Bellerive, 1943
This motorcyclist wears a black-finished M1935 French Army motorized troops' helmet with the Police Nationale badge in painted metal on the front **(see Plate D2a)**. The M1936 Police enlisted ranks' uniform of mounted troops' pattern is in police-blue, with the *francisque*-and-branches badge on the kite-shaped collar patches. The GMR left sleeve badge is in bronze metal; the coloured badge on his right breast pocket is that of his unit, one of three 'Groupes Limagne' (Nos. 63–65) headquartered at Bellerive. In addition to his holstered revolver he carries an 8mm M1892/1916 Berthier carbine.

C3: *Gardien*, April 1944
By this date many GMR men were wearing this popular form of field uniform. The only things that identify this man as a policeman are the Police Nationale badge on his black-painted M1926 Adrian helmet, and the black necktie. He displays no insignia on his brown leather *blouson* jacket, which is worn with an Army khaki shirt, M1941 trousers, gaiters and boots. His weapons are the same as those carried by C2 above.

D: POLICE & SECURITY UNITS, 1942–44
D1: *Sous-brigadier, Garde des Communications*, 1942
This junior NCO of the rail security service displays its badge – a white dagger and gearwheel on a black shield topped with a tricolour bar – painted on his M1926 helmet. This type of navy-blue tunic, of inferior quality and cut, was known as the *surveillance*; note this service's plain mid-green shoulder straps. The collar patches of the same colour are of diamond shape rather than the more usual 'kite', and bear a stylized red 'GC'; they were piped in white for the ranks of *brigadier* and *sous-brigadier*. His exact rank is indicated by the single red 'pip' on the white-piped, five-sided green tab above each cuff. His *culottes* also have green seam-piping.

D2: *Gardien, Groupes Mobiles de Réserve*; Clermont-Ferrand, May 1944
Again, the M1935 motorized troops' helmet with a painted Police badge **(see 2a)** is worn, though here with a conventional narrow chinstrap. This is another field uniform seen in use by the Mobile Reserve Groups shortly before the Normandy landings. The tunic is an economy pattern of the Army's M1941 khaki *vareuse*, worn here with the armoured crew M1935 *salopettes* in khaki canvas, gathered and strapped at the ankle. The black collar patches (and buttons) display the *francisque*-and-branches badge, and his rank is identified by the two yellow inverted chevrons on a backing of police-blue above each cuff, complete with a triangle of blue 'in-fill'. He wears the unit badge of GMR Groupe No. 31 'Auvergne' high on the right breast, and opposite it the ribbon of the 1940 Croix des Combattants. His weapons are an 8mm M1892 revolver and a 7.5mm MAS36 rifle.

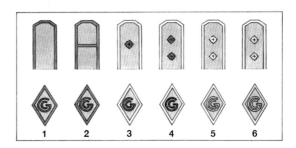

Rank insignia of the Gardes des Communications. The top row illustrates the cuff tabs, the second row the associated collar patches. The field of all insignia was mid-green:

(1) *Gardes de 3e & 2e classe*, red piping and 'GC'; (2) *Garde de 1ère classe*, red piping and 'GC'; (3) *Sous-brigadier* and (4) *Brigadier*, white piping, red 'GC', 1 & 2 red stars; (5) *Sous-chef de Secteur* and *Chef de Secteur*, white piping, white 'GC', 1 & 2 white stars; (6) *Commandant de Secteur* and *Chef de Groupe*, yellow piping, yellow 'GC', 1 & 2 yellow stars.

(Drawings by Adam Hook)

D3: Motorcyclist, *Garde du Maréchal*; Vichy, September 1943

This member of the motorcycle company of Pétain's personal guard battalion is on duty outside his residence in the Hôtel du Parc in the capital of the former Unoccupied Zone. On the M1933 motorcyclists' helmet, with visors front and back and external pads, he displays the Garde's badge: a *francisque* with *tricolore* blades and the shaft as a blue-and-gold marshal's baton, set on a silver flaming shell bearing 'E' and 'F' for 'État Francais'. His black leather three-quarter length coat and matching *culottes* are worn with knee-high gaiters, and white gauntlet gloves. On sentry duty, he is armed with a revolver and a MAS36 rifle with fixed bayonet. He has one blackened M1935 cartridge pouch on his belt, which is fastened with a white-metal buckle bearing the same design as the helmet badge.

E: *MILICE FRANÇAISE*, 1943–44

E1: *Milicien, Francs-gardes permanentes*, April 1944

This Afro-Caribbean militiaman shipped to France from the French Antilles is wearing the full-time *Milicien*'s basic uniform of an M1941 *vareuse* and straight trousers in police-blue wool, the latter bloused over blackened M1941 gaiters and boots. The M1926 helmet, painted black, has an applied white metal badge – the Milice's *gamma* in a pierced circle. The plain shoulder straps indicate the lowest rank; the 'kite'-shaped collar patches have double silver-grey piping at the upper edges, and bear the unit numeral '1'. The only other insignia is the ubiquitous right pocket badge of the circled *gamma*. On street duty in a city, he carries a MAS36 rifle.

E2: Officer candidate; Uriage, summer 1943

This volunteer is identifiable as an officer candidate under instruction at the Milice training school at Uriage by the German-type removable shoulder straps, in white with black stitching, worn on his khaki shirt when in summer shirtsleeve order. The Army shirt and black ski-type trousers reflect the origins of the Milice in the Service d'Ordre Légionnaire (SOL) of the Légion Française des Combattants (see Plate A3). Characteristic Milice features are the large beret of 'Alpine' or 'Fortress' shape, here in midnight-blue with a white-metal badge, and the buckled-on brassard. Although he habitually carries a holstered revolver, here he is relaxing between classes with a French-language edition of the German armed forces' magazine *Signal*.

E3: *Milicien, Francs-gardes non-permanentes*, summer 1943

A part-time *Milicien* on street duty in a town, he wears a typical mix of clothing: an M1926 helmet with a white-painted badge; a khaki uniform shirt with a cloth right-breast badge, the plain blue shoulder straps of the lowest rank, and a Milice brassard; and civilian trousers and 'wing-tip' shoes. By this date he needs a sidearm for self-protection. He is gathering up for destruction copies of the Resistance newspaper *Défense de la France* which was produced and circulated for Bastille Day, 14 July 1943.

F: *MILICE FRANÇAISE*, 1943–44

F1: *Milicien, Francs-gardes permanentes*, autumn 1943

This relaxed barracks gate-guard wears a more rarely seen variant of the police-blue uniform illustrated as Plate E1. Here a waist-length *blouson* replaces the four-pocket *vareuse*; the only insignia is a small enamelled *gamma*

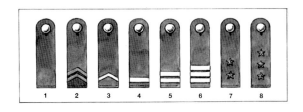

Rank insignia of *francs-gardes permanentes*, Milice Française. All rank distinctions were on police-blue shoulder straps. (1) *Franc-garde*; (2) *Chef de main*, two red chevrons; (3) *Chef de dizaine*, yellow-gold chevron; (4) *Chef de trentaine*, yellow-gold bar; (5) *Chef de centaine*, 2 yellow-gold bars; (6) *Chef de cohorte*, 3 yellow-gold bars; (7) *Chef départmental*, 2 yellow-gold stars; (8) *Chef régional*, 3 yellow-gold stars. Adjutants (deputy commanders) at *trentaine*, *centaine* and *cohorte* level wore respectively 1, 2 & 3 silver bars. (Drawings by Adam Hook)

badge of the *francs-gardes* in silver and black, worn on the collar point.

F2: *Milicienne*, 1943

This young woman, fulfilling a much-needed welfare role, is dressed in an Army shirt with a black tie, but her dark blue A-line skirt with buttoned pocket flaps, her rolled-down woollen socks and laced shoes are all civilian items. On the right pocket she displays an enamelled badge worn by the women's section, a white *gamma* on a royal –blue field with a double red edge **(2a)**.

F3: *Milicien, Francs-gardes permanentes*, winter 1943/44

Suffering the miseries of manning a checkpoint on a lonely country road on a freezing night, this full-time militiaman is lucky to have received a double-breasted *capote* greatcoat in police-blue; against the wind and snow he has turned up the collar and unbuttoned the skirts to hang free. The only insignia is the cut-out white-metal *gamma* on his M1926 helmet, and the only equipment a single cartridge pouch for his MAS36 rifle.

G: *MILICE FRANÇAISE*, PARIS, JULY 1944

G1: *Chef de cohorte*; Les Invalides, 1 July

This equivalent to a battalion commander is taking part in the Milice parade held on 1 July at Les Invalides following the mobilization of all *francs-gardes*; he is in the 'at ease' drill position. He wears an 'Alpine'-style beret, M1941 tunic (and straight trousers) all in police-blue. His rank is indicated by the three gold braid bars on his shoulder straps, his unit by the silver '7' on his collar patches, and his extensive World War I service by his medal-ribbon bar.

G2: *Chef de trentaine*; Les Invalides, 1 July

This platoon commander is acting as a standard-bearer for the 1 July parade. His rank is identified by the single gold bar on the shoulder straps of the same police-blue M1941 uniform as worn by his battalion commander, complete with blackened gaiters and boots. On his left pocket he displays the *gamma*-and-sword badge of a graduate of the Milice leadership school at Uriage **(2a)**.

G3: *Chef de dizaine*; Champs-Élysées, 2 July

Pictured parading through central Paris on the day following

June 1944: this *Milicien* guarding a government building carries a Sten Mk II SMG and wears M1941 uniform in police-blue, with khaki shirt and black tie. The only insignia is the *gamma* badge on his right breast pocket, though he does display a medal ribbon on his left breast – probably marking him as a veteran of the 1940 campaign. (Bundesarchiv, Bild 101I-720-0318-06/photo: Koll)

the ceremony at Les Invalides, this newly mobilized NCO (note single white chevron on blue shoulder-straps) wears a large Milice beret in police-blue with a khaki M1941 uniform issued from the stores of Vichy's disbanded Armistice Army. A group photo shows much variation in the sizes and shades of berets, from small black or midnight-blue to larger size in slightly lighter police-blue, some with and some lacking badges. The *francs-gardes* pictured also wear varying models of khaki trousers and gaiters. All, however, seem to carry

British small arms captured by the German or Vichy authorities from air-drops intended for the Resistance, and released to the *permanentes* from June 1944 to make up for the failure of the Milice's 1943 procurement programme. This NCO is armed with a Sten Mk II sub-machine gun, but for lack of suitable pouches he is reduced to carrying its magazines in his tunic pocket.

H: *MILICE FRANÇAISE*, JULY 1944

H1: *Franc-garde permanente, Groupe Spécial de Sécurité*

This *port-fanion* from the Milice's elite Special Security Group presents arms, wearing the M1941 uniform in police-blue with the addition of white gauntlets for parade. As well as the *gamma* badge on his right pocket he wears on the left the GS's unit shield **(1a)**. The death's-head and initials are repeated on the pennant flown from a rod in the bayonet-tube of his MAS36 rifle, with the word '*Devant*' ('Ahead' or 'In Front'). The Special Group was an understrength *centaine* commanded by Joannès Tomasi, a decorated veteran of the Spanish Foreign Legion and a fervent admirer of Gen Franco. Its official role was to provide security and a guard of honour for Darnand, but it was fully motorized, so also became very active in anti-Resistance fighting. It took part in operations in Limousin, the Auvergne, the Dordogne, and the Annecy and Lyon areas, and lost about 20 per cent casualties. The remainder eventually escaped to Germany, where almost all of them joined the Waffen-SS.

H2: *Chef de dizaine, Francs-gardes permanentes,* Burgundy

In July 1944 the Milice sent two incomplete 100-man companies (*centaines*) from Paris to Dijon in Burgundy, an area where they had only ever managed to raise a platoon (*trentaine*) locally. Given the failure of Milice logistics, the Germans opened for them French Army stores in the Southern Zone. This sergeant from the Île-de-France thus wears entirely M1941 Army gear, apart from his modest-sized midnight-blue beret, police-blue shoulder straps of rank, and a black 'Sam Browne' belt. He has a captured Sten Mk II and a No. 36 grenade, but again, in the absence of suitable pouches, he has to carry magazines thrust into the front of his tunic. Slung behind his hips for a short local operation are an old World War I *etui-musette* haversack, and a privately acquired binocular case. Khaki M1926 helmets were also occasionally carried, with painted or applied *gamma* badges.

H3: *Franc-garde permanente,* Rennes

Deployed in Brittany in the aftermath of the Normandy landings, this *Milicien* shows the rear of the M1941 uniform; note the yoke seams, and the buttoning belt loops attached on each side. Though by this date the absence of numbered collar patches and of sleeve patches was common, this man still displays the traditional Breton black-on-white *hermine* heraldic pattern on a left-sleeve shield. In the absence of other equipment he carries slung round his body an M1935 French Army *musette*, with outer pockets for LMG magazines (when worn as part of the full Y-strap and pack equipment, this was clipped to hang below the belt at the rear). Like many *francs-gardes* deployed in Northern France, he is armed with a captured British .303in Lee-Enfield No. 4 Mk I rifle.

INDEX

Figures in **bold** refer to illustrations.